M E G A B I T E S
SHARKS
RIVETING READS FOR CURIOUS KIDS

By
Dr Miranda MacQuitty

Consultant
Dr Kim Dennis-Bryan

Penguin
Random
House

Revised Edition

DK Delhi

Project Art Editor Mansi Agrawal
Editors Vatsal Verma, Upamanyu Das
Managing Editor Kingshuk Ghoshal
Managing Art Editor Govind Mittal
DTP Designers Jaypal Chauhan,
Mohammad Rizwan, Vikram Singh
Senior DTP Designer Harish Aggarwal
Pre-Production Manager Balwant Singh
Production Manager Pankaj Sharma
Jacket Designer Tanya Mehrotra

DK London

Managing Editor Rachel Fox
Managing Art Editor Owen Peyton Jones
Production Editor Gillian Reid
Production Controller Laura Andrews
Jacket Design Development Manager Sophia MTT
Publisher Andrew MacIntyre
Associate Publishing Director Liz Wheeler
Art Director Karen Self
Publishing Director Jonathan Metcalf

First Edition

Editor Lucy Hurst
Designer Polly Appleton
Senior Editor Fran Jones
Senior Art Editor Stefan Podhorodecki
Category Publisher Jayne Parsons
Managing Art Editor Jacquie Gulliver
Picture Researcher Jo Haddon
DK Pictures Rose Horridge and Sarah Mills
Production Erica Rosen
DTP Designer Siu Yin Ho
Jacket Designer Dean Price

This edition published in 2021
First published in Great Britain in 2002 by
Dorling Kindersley Limited
DK, One Embassy Gardens, 8 Viaduct Gardens,
London, SW11 7BW

The authorised representative in the EEA is
Dorling Kindersley Verlag GmbH. Arnulfstr. 124,
80636 Munich, Germany

The CIP catalogue record for this book is available from the British Library.
ISBN: 978-0-2415-2657-6

Printed and bound in the UK

For the curious

www.dk.com

Note to Parents
Every effort has been made to ensure that the information in this book is as up-to-date as possible at the time of
going to press. The internet, by its very nature, is liable to change. Homepages and website content is constantly
being updated, as well as website addresses. In addition, websites may contain material or links to material that may
be unsuitable for children. The publishers, therefore, cannot accept responsibility for any third party websites or
any material contained in or linked to the same or for any consequences arising from use of the internet; nor can
the publishers guarantee that any website or urls featured in this book will be as shown. Parents are strongly
advised to ensure that access to the internet by children is supervised by a responsible adult.

CONTENTS

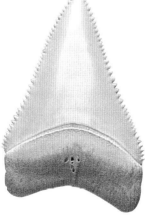

INTRODUCTION

A fin slicing through water, jaws armed with razor-sharp teeth, and awesome senses – no wonder sharks seem frightening. There is, however, much more to sharks than this typical image. Travel into the world of these skilful hunters to discover how they use their powerful bodies to hunt prey. Also take the opportunity to learn about less ferocious sharks and other sea creatures with the skill to kill.

Do sharks deserve their reputation as bloodthirsty killers? People who study sharks certainly don't think so. There are at least 500 extant (or living) species of shark and most of them are harmless to humans. In the pages that follow you'll find out how sharks have earned their deadly reputation, but how it's actually people who pose the biggest threat to shark survival. Learn how sharks have a flexible skeleton and rough outer skin that makes them different from other fish. Discover, too, that sharks range in size from a massive 15 m (49 ft) to one that would fit into the palm of an adult's hand.

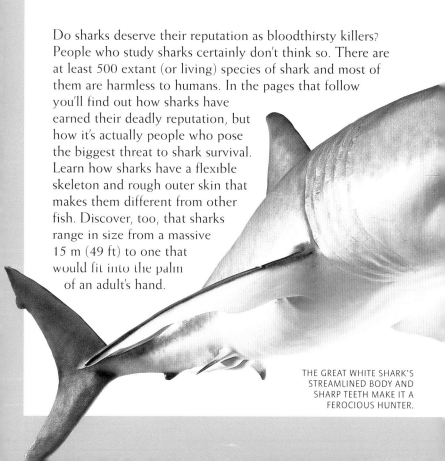

THE GREAT WHITE SHARK'S STREAMLINED BODY AND SHARP TEETH MAKE IT A FEROCIOUS HUNTER.

These creatures have superb senses to track down prey, with an extraordinary ability to detect the smell of blood and the sound of splashing from a distance. Find out about shark teeth and how they are perfectly designed for grasping and biting their favourite foods. How sharks mate is revealed, along with how they give birth.

See an amazing array of shark relatives from stingrays to sawfish. Learn about other mysterious sea creatures from venomous fish and stinging jellies to the weird-looking monsters of the deep.

RAYS ARE CLOSELY RELATED TO SHARKS, BUT HAVE MANY DIFFERENCES TOO.

All sea creatures are under threat. The balance of sea life is altered by overfishing, while chemicals and oil spills poison marine animals and plants. See what you can do to help at the end of the book. The more we learn about the sea, the more we will respect and cherish it.

Miranda MacQuitty

MEET THE SHARKS

Most people would rather not come face to face with a shark, which isn't surprising. They are sophisticated hunters with remarkable senses and bigger brains than most other fish. Most also sport a scary set of teeth! A shark's streamlined shape and powerful body helps it to speed through the water like a torpedo. You can think of adult sharks as the lions or tigers of the sea – the top predators – with few enemies apart from people.

A different kind of fish

One of the first things you need to know about sharks is how they differ from other fish.

For example, sharks have a skeleton made of strong, flexible cartilage – just like the bendy bits inside your ears and nose. Most other fish, such as tuna, have heavier, more rigid, bony skeletons. Some parts of a shark's skeleton are less flexible than others. The backbone is reinforced with strengthening minerals, and is a strong framework for muscles to work against. Teeth are strong too, being made of dentine coated by a hard enamel-like substance.

Sharks have a tough protective skin covered with toothlike scales, called dermal denticles, instead of the flat scales that you see on bony fish. Denticles can be shed and grown again – just like a shark's teeth. If you were to run your hand from tail to head of a shark, it's skin would feel like sandpaper.

A BLUE SHARK SWIMS OFF THE AZORES, IN THE MID-ATLANTIC OCEAN.

ELECTRON MICROSCOPE IMAGE OF THE SKIN OF A DOGFISH WITH ITS COVERING OF DENTICLES

WEIRD WORLD

SHARKS HAVE BEEN SWIMMING
IN THE OCEAN FOR ABOUT
400 MILLION YEARS – THAT
MEANS THEY WERE HERE ABOUT
200 MILLION YEARS BEFORE
THE DINOSAURS.

Shark gills

Sharks also have a different system of breathing. Like all fish, a shark breathes by taking water in through its mouth and passing it over its gills. These do the same job as your lungs, extracting oxygen and passing it into the bloodstream.

But instead of having flaps over their gills, sharks have gill slits. Water streams out through these slits, which you can see between the shark's head and its front fins. There are exceptions to this. Sharks that lie flat on the bottom of the ocean, such as angel sharks, can take in water through a hole behind their eye, called a spiracle, and then pass it out through their gills. This prevents their gills from clogging up with sand – ouch!

THIS HUGE WHALE SHARK GLIDES ALONG THE AUSTRALIAN COAST. DESPITE ITS LARGE SIZE, THE LIGHT CARTILAGE SKELETON AND OILY LIVER OF THE WHALE SHARK HELP KEEP IT IN MID-WATER.

GILL SLITS

Shark fins

As they cruise along, the rigid fins of a shark control and power their movement. Water passing over the front fins – called pectorals – lifts the shark up at the front. This has the same effect as air passing over an aeroplane wing. These fins are also used for steering. To propel a shark forwards, its tail fin beats from side to side. At the same time, the remaining fins act as stabilizers, preventing it from rolling over in the water.

Sink or swim

That is fine while the shark is moving, but if it's not swimming it would gradually sink. This is because sharks are heavier than water. Sharks can't adjust their buoyancy like bony fish that have a gas-filled swim bladder (like a balloon) inside them. Instead sharks have a large oily liver which, coupled with a light cartilaginous skeleton, helps them stay in mid-water. Because oil is lighter than water, the liver lifts the shark up towards the surface.

Sharks that spend a lot of time at the surface, such as whale sharks and basking sharks, have massive livers that are like big floats. This allows them to swim slowly without sinking.

Great and small

These shark features relate to most sharks, but within the shark world there is a great variety of species – more than 500 in fact. Of these, there is no contest over which is the largest shark in the ocean – it's the whale shark, which also happens to be the world's largest fish. It can grow to more than 12.65 m (41.5 ft) long. Luckily for us, these giants are interested in eating plankton, not people! The second largest

ribbontail catshark, and the American pocket shark are the next smallest.

Fast sharks

Neither the biggest nor smallest are the fastest sharks. This honour goes to the great white, porbeagle, mako, and salmon shark, which all have crescent-shaped tail fins. A keel

THE FASTEST SHARKS ARE STREAMLINED LIKE TORPEDOES.

shark, the basking shark, grows to about 10 m (33 ft), which is still enormous.

At the other end of the scale, the record for the world's smallest shark is currently held by the dwarf lantern shark, which can fit in the palm of an adult's hand. The spined pygmy shark, the pygmy

DORSAL FIN STOPS THE SHARK FROM ROLLING ONTO ITS SIDE.

KEEL MAKES SHARK STREAMLINED

CRESCENT-SHAPED TAIL FIN

PELVIC FIN

PECTORAL FIN

running along the narrow base of the tail helps to make these sharks even more streamlined.

Another feature of fast sharks is that they keep their body temperature higher than the surrounding water. Staying warm probably helps their muscles to work better. This increases the shark's swimming speed, so it can catch quick prey such as squid and seals.

The fastest shark of all is the shortfin mako that reaches speeds of up to 68 kph (42 mph). Not much compared to a sports car you may think,

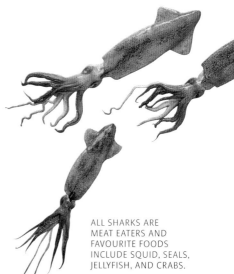

ALL SHARKS ARE MEAT EATERS AND FAVOURITE FOODS INCLUDE SQUID, SEALS, JELLYFISH, AND CRABS.

THE GREAT WHITE SHARK IS ONE OF THE FASTEST IN THE OCEAN. IT USES A BURST OF SPEED TO CHASE AND CATCH PREY.

but water is 800 times denser than air, so it is much harder to move through.

Jumping sharks

Some sharks move so fast, they can leap right out of the water! They may use this skill to try and escape from a fishing line, or when chasing prey. The mako can leap 6 m (18 ft) out of the water. But, most amazing is the leap of the hefty great white shark as it hunts seal pups off Seal Island, South Africa. It gathers speed by charging up through the water, surprising the pups from below. The force carries the shark – and the unfortunate seal – right out of the water!

However fast or slow, big or small, each shark is perfectly adapted to successfully hunt, kill, and devour its prey.

WHERE SHARKS LIVE

You could swim in any of the world's oceans, from the sunny surface and shallows to the dark depths, and be in shark territory. A few types of shark even make their homes in lakes and rivers. To blend in with their surroundings, many sharks rely on camouflage to give them an element of surprise when hunting their prey.

Hot or cold water?
Different types of shark are adapted to different water temperatures and generally

The starry smoothhound and horn sharks like living in water that's not too hot or too cold. The starry smoothhound is

THE STARRY SMOOTHHOUND SHARK LIKES LIVING IN TEMPERATE WATERS.

need to stay within the right area to survive. Some like to swim where it's warm, such as the whale sharks that live in the tropical waters of the Atlantic, Pacific, and Indian oceans.

But other sharks, such as the Greenland shark, prefer cold water. In winter they live in the icy waters of the Arctic Ocean and neighbouring areas. In summer when the water gets warmer, they head for deeper, colder waters.

WHITETIP REEF SHARKS RESTING IN A CAVE
OFF THE REVILLAGIGEDO ISLANDS, MEXICO

found off the coast of
Northern Europe and
the Mediterranean.

Near the shore
Sharks have never been the
easiest of animals to watch
or study, and those we get to
know best are the ones that
come close to land. Female
lemon sharks, for example,
come into sheltered water near
the coast in the Bahamas to give
birth. This is one of the rare
occasions when people have
seen shark pups being born.

Tiger sharks also come close
to land in order to feed on
young albatrosses in Pacific
Island lagoons. Any young
birds that misjudge their

first flight are snapped up
if they falter and tumble
into the water.

Reef sharks
Snorkellers and scuba divers
may see some of the beautiful
reef sharks that hunt around
corals. The blacktip reef shark
lives in the shallow water over
reefs and in coral lagoons,
while the grey reef shark
lives in deeper water, such
as along channels and outer
reefs. The whitetip reef shark
rests under ledges and in
caves during the day. It
generally hunts at night,
poking its snout around corals
in search of fish, octopuses,
crabs, and lobsters.

Sea floor dwellers

Many types of shark live on or near the bottom of shallow coastal waters. Horn sharks rest together in rocky crevices during the day, and then at night they look for food such as shellfish on the sea floor.

Nurse sharks could be seen as the lazy sharks because they spend much of the day resting on the sandy sea floor, often near coral reefs. When they get peckish, they are like giant vacuum cleaners, sucking prey off the sea floor or from between rocks. Longtailed carpetsharks have extra flexible bodies and can use their pectoral and pelvic fins to clamber over coral, into crevices, and between rock pools.

Camouflaged sharks

Other sea floor sharks are exceptionally flat – so much so that you'd think they were part of the sea floor! Being flat helps some sharks stay camouflaged. For example, wobbegongs and angel sharks are just the right shape to lie there, ready to ambush any unwary fish or crab

WEIRD WORLD
WOBBEGONG SHARKS LIVE IN SHALLOW COASTAL AREAS AROUND AUSTRALIA, PARTS OF INDONESIA, AND THE WESTERN PACIFIC OCEAN – AS FAR NORTH AS JAPAN.

THE TASSELLED WOBBEGONG LIVES ON THE OCEAN FLOOR – JUST LIKE A SEA CARPET. CAN YOU MAKE OUT ITS EYES ON TOP OF ITS HEAD?

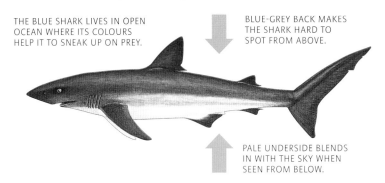

THE BLUE SHARK LIVES IN OPEN OCEAN WHERE ITS COLOURS HELP IT TO SNEAK UP ON PREY.

BLUE-GREY BACK MAKES THE SHARK HARD TO SPOT FROM ABOVE.

PALE UNDERSIDE BLENDS IN WITH THE SKY WHEN SEEN FROM BELOW.

passing by. Wobbegongs have elaborate skin patterns and leafy bits of skin around their heads which allow them to blend in with weed-covered rocks or coral reefs. Angel sharks go one step further by becoming part of the sea floor. They shuffle down into the sand and become harder to see.

Open ocean

Sharks that live further out to sea also use camouflage. The sharks living in the surface waters, such as the blue shark, pelagic thresher, and mako, have bluish-grey backs and light-coloured bellies. Their backs blend in with the sea when viewed from above, and their bellies blend in with the sky when viewed from below. This colouring gives them a chance to approach their prey without being seen.

Deep-water sharks

If you took a submersible down to the depths, you probably wouldn't see a shark unless you

equally strange. Its long snout, beady eyes, and pinkish-grey skin look spooky! It swims about hunting other creatures deep in the Atlantic, Pacific, and Indian oceans.

To the surface and back

Some sharks live in deep water during the day, and then travel up to feed in shallower mid-water at night. These sharks then feed near the surface, using the cover of darkness to surprise their prey.

MANY DEEP-SEA SHARKS ARE HIDDEN BY THEIR DARK COLOURS.

put out bait. Few sharks can live in deep water as there just isn't enough food for them to eat. Occasionally, though, sharks have been spotted at depths of more than 3 km (1.9 miles).

Sharks that do live in deep water don't always look like typical sharks. For example, the birdbeak dogfish has a long snout and huge eyes that help it to see in the gloomy water. Another deep-water shark, the goblin shark, looks

The spined pygmy shark does this to follow its dinner – squid and fish – which makes the same journey.

Another shark with similar habits is the megamouth, which lives more than 200 m (660 ft) below the ocean's surface. At night, it travels slowly upwards to feed on shrimplike krill, jellyfish, and other tasty morsels drifting near the surface waters. The megamouth is one of the rarest sharks, and was only

A BIRDBEAK DOGFISH PHOTOGRAPHED NEAR THE SEABED OFF MADEIRA ISLAND, PORTUGAL

PORT JACKSON SHARKS TRAVEL TO SHALLOW WATERS TO MATE AND LAY EGGS.

discovered in the 1970s. It's unusual that such a large shark – more than 5 m (16 ft) in length – was not discovered for such a long time.

Home and away

As you'd probably expect from such powerful swimmers, sharks can cover long distances across the ocean, not just up and down. Some sharks travel a long way in search of a mate, to find the right water temperature, or for food. The Port Jackson shark – a type of horn shark – travels to shallow water each year to mate in its favourite breeding grounds. Some sand tiger sharks migrate to warmer waters in winter and return again in summer.

Blue sharks are the most travelled. They do a round-trip from one side of the Atlantic Ocean to

the other for feeding and breeding. We know sharks migrate because scientists have tracked them. They collect data by tagging sharks and recording further sightings of them to show where the sharks travel. Sharks can also be followed using electronic tags that send out signals. Gradually, scientists are revealing the secrets of shark migration.

Adaptable sharks

Sharks seem to live almost everywhere in the ocean, and some species can even live in

MARINE BIOLOGISTS CAN DOWNLOAD INFORMATION ABOUT WHERE A SHARK TRAVELS ONTO A COMPUTER.

19

rivers and lakes. The bull shark has been found 4,000 km (2,485 miles) up the Amazon. It has also been spotted in the Mississippi in the USA, and the Zambezi in Africa. Bull sharks swim upriver from the sea, and are able to move from sea to freshwater by regulating salt and other substances in their blood. Some sharks swim so far up rivers that they reach lakes, such as Lake Nicaragua in Central America.

Finding river sharks is a challenge. Some, such as the speartooth shark, are endangered because their river habitats are threatened by development.

Travelling companions
Wherever a shark goes, a little band of travelling companions joins in. It is hard to imagine seeking out the company of sharks, but pilotfish and young golden trevally fish like to tag along. By swimming next to big sharks, these small fish are safe from other big fish that might eat them. Sounds risky, but they're swift enough to keep clear of a shark's jaws.

Shark suckers
Even though the remora fish can swim perfectly well, catching a ride on a shark saves energy. They have ridged suckers on their heads that they use to clamp on to large sharks. Apart from free transport, remoras also get to snack on any bits of food that don't make it into the shark's mouth.

Small types of remora act as cleaners by nibbling skin parasites off sharks. Some even venture into whale sharks' mouths where they probably remove parasites that irritate the shark. Some will even eat the shark's poo.

Whether harmful or helpful to the shark, its fellow travellers are well suited to their particular way of making a living.

WEIRD WORLD
NOT ALL CREATURES THAT TRAVEL WITH SHARKS ARE FRIENDLY. PARASITES, SUCH AS THESE SHRIMPLIKE COPEPODS, SCRAPE AWAY AT A SHARK'S SKIN AND EAT IT, IRRITATING THE SHARK.

REMORAS ATTACH THEMSELVES TO THE UNDERSIDE OF A WHALE SHARK.

SUPERB SENSES

One of the main reasons sharks are so successful is their sophisticated senses. Sharks smell, taste, touch, see, and hear, but can also pick up electrical signals generated by their prey. A shark's senses are well-tuned, whether it's a speedy hunter, a lie-in-wait predator, or a sluggish seeker of food along the sea floor. Sharks also use senses to identify threats, meet a mate, and find their way.

Sense of smell
Smell is an important shark sense. Like us, sharks smell with their nostrils, but they don't breathe through them. Instead, sea water streams through a shark's nostrils as it swims along, bringing chemical clues about what's in the water. At the back of the nostrils there

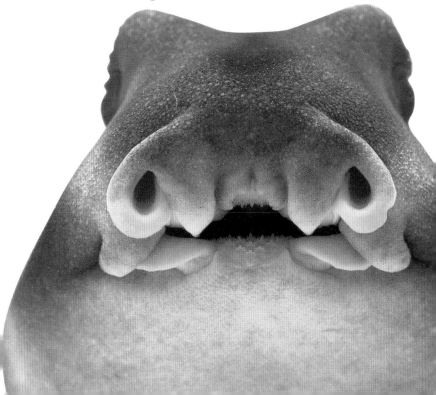

are baglike structures that contain leafy folds. As the sea water flows up the nostrils and between the folds, chemicals in the water bind to the surface of the folds. These chemicals trigger nerve signals that zip off to the shark's brain for processing, telling the shark which of its favourite foods is swimming nearby.

Smells in water

A shark's sense of smell is so good it can detect tiny concentrations of blood that have been

A SHARK USES ITS SHARP SENSE OF SMELL TO DETECT BLEEDING OR INJURED ANIMALS THAT MAKE EASY PREY.

SMELL IS ONE OF THE MAIN SENSES SHARKS USE TO FIND FOOD.

diluted more than a million times. Sharks can smell and identify many other things too – for example, tests have shown that the blacktip reef shark can smell one drop of fish extract in the equivalent of an Olympic-sized swimming pool. But it depends when it last ate. Amazingly, the hungrier a shark, the better it is

HORN SHARKS, LIKE THIS ONE, HAVE WELL-DEVELOPED NOSTRILS AND A KEEN SENSE OF SMELL.

at detecting the smell of fish. A shark may smell an injured animal hundreds of metres away. Once the smell registers in the shark's brain it thinks "goody, grub's up", and swims back and forth following the

23

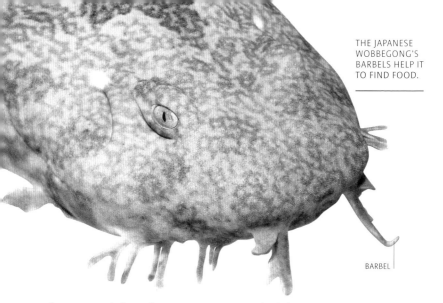

THE JAPANESE
WOBBEGONG'S
BARBELS HELP IT
TO FIND FOOD.

BARBEL

direction of the odour,
until it homes in on the
injured animal.

Taste buds
Smell works at a distance, but
for a shark to really know if it
likes something, it has to take
a bite or attempt to swallow
it. Once there's food inside
its mouth, a shark uses the
taste buds in its mouth and
gullet. Sharks do have a tongue,
called a basihyal, but it lacks
taste buds and is usually non-
functional. Sharks are not
known for their table manners,
and if it doesn't like the taste of
what it's eaten – it spits it out.

Touchy feely
Some sharks may be able to
taste and feel using a pair of
feelers, called barbels, on the

end of their snout. Nurse
sharks, bamboo sharks, and
wobbegongs are among those
that have barbels. These are
very useful for feeling around
for buried prey, and possibly
tasting it too if they have taste
receptors on their barbels.
   Sharks also have nerve
endings under their skin that
are sensitive to touch. So it's

WEIRD WORLD
SOME FISH ARE SPECIALLY ADAPTED
SO THAT THEIR PREDATORS,
INCLUDING SHARKS, FIND THEM
DISTASTEFUL. FOR EXAMPLE, THE
FINLESS SOLE COATS ITSELF WITH
A TOXIC SLIME. ITS BITTER TASTE
DETERS OTHER FISH FROM
EATING IT.

never a good idea to poke a shark! These nerve endings can gather information about the surroundings even when other senses cannot, and keep the shark aware of other predators and prey in the area.

Eye spy

As well as great senses of smell, taste, and touch, sharks also have exceptional eyesight. A shark's eyes are usually located on each side of its head, although some sea-floor dwelling sharks have eyes on the top of their heads. Hammerhead sharks have eyes on the far edges of their T-shaped heads, which they swing from side to side for a better view.

THIS IS A CLOSE-UP OF A NURSE SHARK'S EYE. THE IRIS (WHITE) CONTRACTS OR EXPANDS TO ALLOW IN DIFFERENT LEVELS OF LIGHT.

SOME SHRIMPS MAKE
SNAPPING NOISES THAT
MAY ATTRACT THE
ATTENTION OF SHARKS.

Although they are underwater, sharks can see the intensity of different shades, but are thought to be colour blind as they cannot see all colours. Deep-water sharks have adapted to see well in blue light, because blue is the part of the light spectrum that penetrates the deepest in the ocean.

Night vision

Sharks have excellent eyesight in the dark, and see ten times better than we can in dim light. This means they can hunt during the half-light of dawn and dusk, or at night. Sharks can see well in the dark because a mirror-like layer at the back of each eye bounces light rays back, making the most of the available light. This reflection of light also means that if you shine a light on a shark's eyes in the dark, they light up yellow or green like the eyes of a cat.

Daytime sight

Sharks also see well during the day, and have pupils that adapt to different amounts of light, just like ours. When the iris opens up, the pupil gets larger and lets in more light, but if the iris closes, the pupil gets smaller and lets in less light. This is unusual in fish.

Shut eye

Another thing about shark sight is that some, including the blue and lemon sharks, have a third eyelid that draws across the eye. They close this third eyelid when feeding to protect the eye – their normal eyelids don't close. The great white shark doesn't have a third eyelid but it does roll its eyes back in their sockets when attacking prey. This protects the more delicate front part of the eye from damage if the prey pokes the shark in the eye while struggling to escape.

Noisy sea

Seeing may be different underwater but so is hearing. This is because sounds travel better in water than on land. The sea is full of weird noises, such as shrimps snapping or whales singing. Sharks don't make many noises themselves, apart from crunching up their prey with their big teeth. But sharks use their sense of hearing all the time to help them find their prey. They can hear sounds from more than 250 m (820 ft) away, and are especially sensitive to the sound of splashing made by an injured fish or mammal.

Ear inside

In order to hear these sounds, sharks have ears. However, you might not recognize them as they don't have the outer ear flaps of cartilage that our ears have. But inside their heads, a shark's inner ear is a bit like ours, except that it is connected to a tiny, fluid-filled canal. This canal opens to the outside on either side of the shark's head. Sound waves travel through the water and down the

WEIRD WORLD

SHARKS ARE BEST AT DETECTING LOW-FREQUENCY SOUNDS, SOME OF WHICH ARE TOO LOW FOR US TO HEAR. THEY CAN'T HEAR THE HIGH-FREQUENCY SOUNDS DOLPHINS MAKE.

canal to the inner ear. Here, sensors send messages to the shark's brain for processing and taking action if necessary.

The inner ear also lets the shark know the position of its body in the water in the same way that our ears help us to balance.

Good vibrations

Like other fish, sharks can detect vibrations in the water. They do this using a line of sensory cells

SOUNDS MADE UNDERWATER MOVE IN WAVES TOWARDS THIS STARRY SMOOTHHOUND SHARK'S EARS.

called a lateral line. This runs along the side of the body, and branches out around the head. Each sense cell sits in an opening that contains tiny hairs. These hairs detect any vibrations in the water. A shark can therefore sense water movement caused by another creature nearby – which might turn out to be prey or a predator. It also helps them avoid bumping into obstacles.

Electric aura

The most amazing sense of all is the shark's ability to detect weak electricial signals made by other creatures. Muscle contractions, nerve signals, and the difference between body fluids and the surrounding sea water generate minuscule amounts of electricity. So every creature has a kind of electric aura – we just can't see it. Sharks sense this electricity through little jelly-filled pores on the head and especially around the mouth. One of the best sharks at detecting weak electricity

is the hammerhead. It has an area dotted with lots of pores under its head.

Using their spark

Sharks use this electrosense, as it is known, to find prey that lives in murky water or is hidden in the sand. Lie-in-wait predators may use their electrosense at night to work out when an animal gets within reach of their swift jaws. Sharks are not alone – a variety of other fish also

HAMMERHEAD SHARKS HAVE A HIGHLY TUNED ELECTROSENSE.

SCALLOPED HAMMERHEAD SHARKS USE ELECTROSENSING TO DETECT LANDMARKS ON THE SEA FLOOR.

have the ability to sense electric auras. They may use electrosensing to communicate with others and to locate mates.

Finding their way

Electrosensing also helps sharks to find their way. By sensing the difference between their own electric aura and Earth's magnetic field, scientists think sharks take a compass reading to keep them travelling in one direction. The electrosensory pores under the head of the scalloped hammerhead are widely placed, so they may even be able to detect different magnetic patterns on the sea floor. These could act as landmarks or even routes a particular area.

The shark's ability to electrosense is important for its survival, but all of its senses are vital when hunting for prey.

JAWS!

The first thing you notice about typical sharks is their teeth – lots of 'em! Imagine seeing row after row of spiky teeth, packed into a huge, powerful jaw, opening up before you as you swim in the sea. Not all sharks will harm humans – but they're all meat eaters at the top of the food chain. Sharks eat in different ways, devouring a variety of food from plankton to seals and other sharks.

Tooth replacement

Sharks are perhaps best known – and feared – for their amazing teeth. Whatever shape or size they are, a shark's teeth make it an efficient killer. What is worse (for their prey) is that a shark has a never-ending supply. New teeth move forwards continuously, as though they are on a conveyor belt. Sharks can lose teeth when biting prey because their teeth are set into their gums but not secured into their jaws, like ours. Every time one is lost, a new one is ready to replace it. And, because new teeth are always larger than the ones they replace, sharks look scarier as they grow older.

Most sharks replace just a few teeth at a time. Scientists observing young lemon sharks in captivity have noticed that it can take about eight days for all of their teeth to be replaced. Other sharks, such as the Greenland shark, shed a whole row of teeth at once, so get a new set of pearly white gnashers every time.

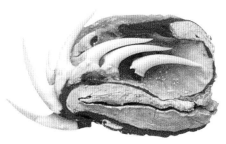

A CROSS-SECTION OF A MAKO SHARK'S JAW SHOWS THE CONVEYOR BELT OF SPIKY NEW TEETH GRADUALLY MOVING FORWARDS.

Types of teeth

Each species of shark is equipped with the right shape of teeth for its favourite food. The curved spiky teeth of the sand tiger and mako shark are great at gripping slippery fish or squid. A fully grown great white shark has triangular, jagged-edged teeth that can carve big chunks of flesh from large animals, such as seals. Some sharks have blunt teeth

WEIRD WORLD

TIGER SHARKS SWALLOW ALL KINDS OF "FOOD" – ONE EVEN HAD A CHICKEN COOP WITH THE REMAINS OF BONES AND FEATHERS INSIDE ITS STOMACH.

that allow them to crunch through the shells of snails, clams, sea urchins, crabs, and lobsters. The dusky smoothhound shark's blunt

A SAND TIGER SHARK HAS VERY SPIKY TEETH TO SPEAR FISH OR SQUID.

teeth are arranged close together for crushing their crab and lobster prey.

Multi-task teeth
But a few sharks aren't content with single-purpose teeth, and have more than one type in

through a turtle's shell due to its large, wide, part-serrated teeth. Tiger sharks will eat all sorts of things, including dead animals and even rubbish.

THE BIGGEST SHARKS ARE GENTLE FILTER-FEEDERS.

their mouths. For example, the sicklefin weasel shark has curved pointed teeth in the lower jaw to grab octopuses, and back-pointing, jagged edged teeth in the upper jaw to slice them up. There are also sharks with different parts to each tooth, such as is seen in the tiger shark. It can dine on soft foods such as jellyfish or crunch

Tiny teeth
Not all sharks have big scary teeth – some no longer need to use theirs at all. The whale shark and basking shark have tiny teeth, especially compared to their gigantic size. They filter small creatures, called plankton, out of the water like a

BULL
SHARK'S TOOTH

GREAT WHITE
SHARK'S TOOTH

TIGER
SHARK'S
TOOTH

BASKING SHARK'S TEETH

MICROSCOPIC
PLANKTON SEEN
MAGNIFIED

A BASKING SHARK
SWIMS WITH ITS MOUTH
OPEN TO CATCH PLANKTON.

Jaw action

So that sharks can open their mouths to feed, they need jaws. These are made of tough cartilage, sometimes reinforced with minerals to make the jaw strong enough to crush hard-shelled prey. Large, powerful muscles slam the jaw shut in an instant around helpless prey. The point of each tooth exerts huge pressure, puncturing the skin or shell of the animal it has caught. Unless the shark lets go, it is impossible for the prey to wriggle free. A shark's mouth lies under its head but it can still take a big bite because its upper jaw is only loosely attached to the skull. The shark's lower jaw

giant sieve. The whale shark can suck in water, while the basking shark swims along with its mouth wide open. Inside the basking shark's mouth, plankton gets trapped in mucus on the long, black, bristly gill rakers in front of the gills. Every couple of minutes, the shark shuts its mouth and squeezes the gill rakers so the whole gooey mass goes down its throat.

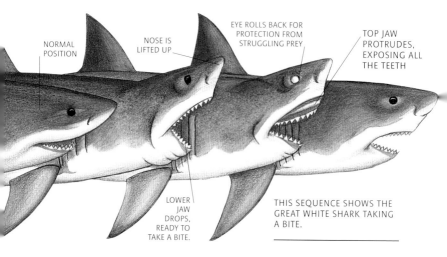

NORMAL POSITION

NOSE IS LIFTED UP

EYE ROLLS BACK FOR PROTECTION FROM STRUGGLING PREY

TOP JAW PROTRUDES, EXPOSING ALL THE TEETH

LOWER JAW DROPS, READY TO TAKE A BITE.

THIS SEQUENCE SHOWS THE GREAT WHITE SHARK TAKING A BITE.

drops, and the upper jaw pushes forwards exposing the teeth. As the upper jaw slams down on prey, the lower jaw moves upwards. Because their jaws push out, sharks can take large bites without choking, unlike us! However, sharks can't chew their food like we do. When eating large prey, they have to shake their heads from side to side to tear off chunks of flesh.

WEIRD WORLD
THE GREAT WHITE SHARK CAN LIFT ITS HEAD OUT OF THE WATER TO CHECK OUT WHAT IS HAPPENING ON THE SURFACE.

Great white feeding
One shark that tears off large chunks of flesh is the great white. It can grow to more than 6 m (20 ft) long, and is the biggest of the hunting sharks. The great white is big enough to eat large prey, such as seals, sea lions, and whale carcasses, animals that have lots of blubber or fat, which provides the energy the shark needs to swim continuously.

The great white usually approaches its victim from below, charging through the water to take an enormous bite of flesh. If the shark decides the animal tastes good, it will attack in earnest. A seal may be carried in the shark's mouth as it swims, and then a chunk of its flesh removed. A great white may let go of an injured animal, and then attack it again, until it dies from loss of blood.

The great hammerhead shark is especially fond of stingrays, and can use its hammer to pin one down while it takes a bite.

A GREAT WHITE ALWAYS HAS AT LEAST 100 FUNCTIONAL TEETH.

Heads and tails

Hammerhead sharks don't eat such large prey as the great white. They hunt fish, squid, and other swimming sea creatures. Hammerheads also seek out rays hiding on the sandy sea floor.

Using the head as a clamp works for hammerheads, but thresher sharks use their long tails when hunting. It is used to herd a shoal of fish together and

A GREAT WHITE SHARK LUNGES FOR BAIT, TEETH AND JAWS READY FOR ACTION.

teeth lie almost flat in the mouth, which means that shelled prey, such as crabs, can be crunched up, and fish cannot escape from the vicelike grip of the shark.

Cookiecutters

The most bizarre feeding technique of all sharks is that of the cookiecutter

A CLOSE-UP VIEW OF A COOKIECUTTER'S MOUTH SHOWS ITS ROW OF SHARP TEETH. IT LEAVES A DISTINCTIVE CIRCULAR WOUND IN ITS PREY.

then "cracked" like a bullwhip to stun or injure the fish, making them easy for the thresher to catch.

Nurse shark suction

The nurse shark is too slow to catch fast fish swimming in mid-water. Instead, it prefers to find fish and other animals close to the bottom, or lurking in rocky crevices. The nurse shark sticks its snout into the crevice, and sucks out its prey like an underwater vacuum cleaner. The backward-pointing

36

shark. It is named after the metal cutters used to punch cookie (biscuit) shapes. Its lower jaw is armed with a vicious set of sharp, triangular teeth. In comparison to its body size, the teeth of the largetooth cookiecutter are twice the size of a great white's.

The cookiecutter latches onto a large fish or a marine mammal, such as a dolphin, with its suckerlike lips. Digging its teeth deep into the skin, the cookiecutter swivels around to take out a plug of flesh. The telltale sign of a cookiecutter's activities are circular wounds on the sides of the animals they have attacked.

Meal times

That's how sharks capture their prey, but did you realize that sharks hunt at different times? Great white sharks often hunt during the day, when seals and sea lions are most active. Many other sharks prefer to hunt in the limited light of dawn, dusk, or at night. Some sharks hunt in a group, such as the spiny dogfish.

Sharks may gather together if attracted to bait or a large dead animal such as a whale. When this happens, shark senses go into

NURSE AND CARIBBEAN REEF SHARKS CLUSTER AROUND BAIT.

A SURFER SHOWS OFF HIS BOARD AFTER A TIGER SHARK ATTACK.

overdrive because of all the blood and food in the water, and they get very excited. Sometimes they attack anything that moves – even some of their pals – in the feeding frenzy.

Hungry for humans?

Sharks eat all sorts of different prey but are we on the menu? For most sharks definitely not. Of the few sharks that attack humans, it is usually a case of mistaken identity or because we've invaded their space. Sharks may even swim strangely to warn divers to back off, just as they would do to another shark on their patch. For example, the grey reef shark opens its mouth, arches it back, and lowers its pectoral fins to warn divers away.

Sometimes though, a person may provoke a shark into biting. An irritated shark may bite if it's being fished out of the water, or if a diver is foolish enough to pull its tail for a joke. If a shark thinks that its life is being threatened, it will defend itself.

Unprovoked attacks may occur in murky water or in the surf, where a shark could mistake human feet or limbs for fish. The shark often takes one bite, and then realizes its mistake and swims away. People may need stitches but aren't usually seriously injured.

Dangerous sharks

But some sharks, particularly the bull shark, tiger shark, and great white, are dangerous and can cause more damage than bad cuts. These big sharks

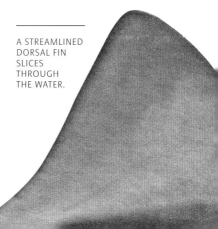

A STREAMLINED DORSAL FIN SLICES THROUGH THE WATER.

swim close to shore where people swim and surf. Here they can really harm a human, even if they don't intend to.

of them died. You are much more likely to drown, be struck by lightning, or die from a bee sting. Most sharks are shy and

YOU'RE MORE LIKELY TO BE KILLED BY LIGHTNING THAN BY A SHARK.

Bull sharks eat all kinds of different prey, from fish to dolphins. They like shallow warm water and tidal creeks – places where they might come across a person. Tiger sharks eat all kinds of things including rubbish. This shows that they are less selective, so may try to eat anything, even people, when they are hungry.

Adult great whites prefer energy-rich fatty food, such as blubber-coated seals and sea lions, to humans. They may attack people surfing near seal colonies because surfers paddling on their boards look like seals to a shark as it swims underneath. Unfortunately, even if a great white doesn't intend to eat a person, one bite can be fatal.

Attacks and safety tips

The International Shark Attack File based in Florida, USA, keeps records of shark attacks. In 2020, there were 57 unprovoked shark attacks on people worldwide, and 10

keep away from us, so the risk of an attack is tiny. But, if you're paddling, swimming, snorkelling, or diving where there could be sharks, it may help to:
• Check with lifeguards, and dive or snorkel instructors about local shark behaviour.
• Make sure you're with other people – sharks are more likely to attack a lone person.
• Avoid being in the water at dawn, dusk, and at night.
• Don't swim if you have an open wound – sharks home in on the smell of blood.
• Don't wear jewellery, as light bouncing off shiny metal might look like the scales of a fish.
• Keep away from places where fish gather, such as in sewage-polluted waters or where people are fishing using bait.
• Don't splash much, and avoid swimming with a splashing dog. Sharks are attracted to the noise.
• Avoid murky water, and wear goggles or a mask so you can see if a shark approaches.

A SHARK IS BORN

Like most animals, male and female sharks get together to produce young. Once the parent sharks court and mate, baby sharks – or pups – develop in three different ways, depending on their species. The first group develop from eggs that their mother has left among seaweed or between rocks. All other sharks grow into pups inside their mother's womb. Of these, one group uses food from their own eggs, and the other group receives food through mum's blood supply – more like mammals than fish!

Finding a mate

Before a female shark can become pregnant she must reach an age when she can mate. In most species, this is any time after the age of six. Mating then occurs every year for some species, but less frequently for those with long pregnancies.

Sharks often swim great distances to breeding areas. Some, such as the Port Jackson shark, return to the same area each year. But because not many people have seen sharks breeding, no one knows where many species go to breed.

But we do know that courtship can be rough for female sharks. Males often swim after females and bite them. Scientists think that this biting may encourage the female to mate.

With large sharks, the male needs to grab hold of the female to mate. As sharks

FEMALE SHARKS HAVE THICK SKINS THAT HELP SURVIVE COURTSHIP BITES.

haven't got limbs, he has to bite her pectoral fin to hang onto her. For this reason, the female blue shark's skin is three times thicker than the male's!

Competing for a mate

For smaller, more flexible sharks, mating is a lot easier. The male can wrap his body around the female instead of biting her. For example, the male lesser spotted dogfish can curl his body around the female. But first he has to "win" her – and there is a lot of competition among the male dogfish.

DURING COURTSHIP, THE MALE WHITETIP REEF SHARK BITES THE FIN OF THE FEMALE.

shed sperm and eggs into the water. Instead, a male shark has to place sperm inside the female's body. He does this using one of the two claspers that lie under his body between the pelvic fins. He rotates one clasper forwards, and then flushes sperm into the female's cloaca – a body opening under her belly. The sperm then fertilize the female's eggs, although some sharks can store the sperm and fertilize their eggs later.

A YOUNG DOGFISH GROWS INSIDE AN EGG BEFORE HATCHING.

Sometimes a female may even need to seek refuge in a cave to escape from all the attention.

Mating sharks

Once the sharks have courted, they mate. This is very different from bony fish, who simply

Once the eggs are fertilized, they start to develop inside the female shark. At this point, things change. Pups of different species will complete their development in one of three ways.

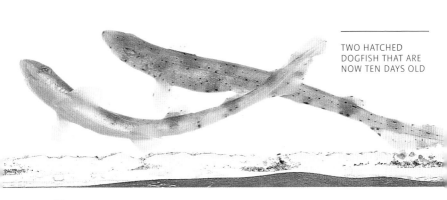

TWO HATCHED DOGFISH THAT ARE NOW TEN DAYS OLD

42

Shark eggs

A few types of shark lay eggs into the water after they are fertilized. They only lay a few large eggs, unlike bony fish who shed thousands of tiny ones. The eggs have tough horny coats, called mermaid's purses, to help protect them. Dogfish egg cases have long curly tendrils at each end that wind around seaweed so they're not washed away. Bamboo,

temperature, the baby shark breaks free of its egg nursery, and begins its life in the ocean.

In the womb

Most sharks don't lay eggs. Instead, they give birth to fully formed little sharks, called pups. There are two ways that the pups grow inside their mother, depending on the type of shark. In some sharks, the embryos feed on the

epaulette, and zebra sharks lay eggs with tufts of sticky, hairlike fibres that anchor them to coral and rocky reefs.

Apart from laying her eggs in the safest place possible, the mother shark does nothing more for her babies, and the father shark is long gone.

A PREGNANT BLACKTIP SHARK SWIMS IN THE PACIFIC OCEAN.

yolk attached to their bellies. When this is used up, they get extra nutrients from fluid secreted into the womb or they eat unfertilized eggs.

Inside the egg

Once the eggs are laid, the baby shark, or embryo, inside develops, feeding on the nutrient-rich yolk attached to its belly. From several weeks to 15 months later, depending on the shark and the water

WEIRD WORLD

FEMALE HORN SHARKS LAY SOFT, SPIRAL-SHAPED EGGS, WHICH THEY PUSH INTO CREVICES. AS THEY HARDEN THE EGGS BECOME SAFELY WEDGED AND HIDDEN FROM VIEW.

THE BAHAMAS IS ONE OF THE FEW PLACES WHERE THE BIRTH OF LEMON SHARKS HAS BEEN SEEN.

Pregnant mums

As well as the two different ways baby sharks grow inside their mums, there is also a variation in the length of time the female shark is pregnant. The bonnethead shark has a short pregnancy of only 4.5–5 months. But most sharks have a pregnancy of at least nine months, the same as human mothers. The spiny dogfish has a pregnancy that lasts up to two years, which is as long or longer than an elephant, and then gives birth to between 10 and 20 pups. Basking shark mums can be pregnant for over three years.

The first pup to hatch inside the sand tiger shark devours some brothers and sisters as hatched embryos, and then feeds on the unfertilized eggs. Finally, only two pups are left – one on each side of the mother's womb. By feasting on their siblings, sand tiger pups grow large, and are more likely to survive once they're born.

Cord connection

The second way pups grow inside their mother occurs in sharks such as hammerheads and lemon sharks. Instead of depending on the yolk for food, the embryos tap into the womb like human babies. Each growing shark – and there can be many – has an umbilical cord that connects it to its mother's blood supply. Blood vessels in the cord bring food and oxygen to each baby, and take away its wastes.

Giving birth

When the time comes to give birth, the female shark generally loses her appetite. This is so she won't be tempted to eat her own pups!

Lemon sharks give birth in shallow water in sheltered lagoons where larger sharks cannot reach them. The pups, so they do not get jammed in the mother's birth canal. Once born, the pups must find food and escape predators all on their own.

The bigger the pup when it is born, the better its chance of survival. The sand tiger, dusky shark, and great white shark's pups are more than

GREAT WHITE SHARK PUPS ARE OVER 1 M (3.3 FT) LONG AT BIRTH.

which are born tail first, swim out to deeper waters two to three years later when about 90 cm (35.4 in) long.

Hammerhead sharks also give birth to pups. Fortunately, their heads are reasonably soft

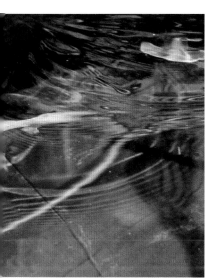

70 cm (28 in) long at birth, already too big for most predators. Lemon shark pups are about 50–60 cm (20–24 in) at birth so must hide away in the safety of mangrove roots to avoid being eaten by other sharks. Whale shark pups are born only 41–61 cm (16–24 in) long – they have a lot of growing to do before they deserve the title of the biggest fish in the sea!

Sharks grow slowly all their lives and it will be a few years until they are ready to have pups of their own. If they're not caught by people or weakened by disease, some can live to a grand old age – even as old as 272 years!

SCALLOPED HAMMERHEAD SHARK PUPS SWIM IN SHALLOW WATER NEAR OAHU, HAWAII.

COUSIN RAY

Sharks are fascinating and mysterious creatures but some of their close relatives are worth finding out about too. Rays and chimaeras are closely related to sharks and are just as intriguing. They have enough similarities – specifically a cartilage skeleton – to be cousins, but plenty of differences too. This side of the family is generally harmless, although some species can give a nasty sting or vicious shock!

Spot the difference

At first glance, most rays don't look anything like sharks. But a closer look shows they have a number of similarities. Like sharks, they have skeletons made of flexible cartilage. Also, they would sink if they stopped swimming, because they don't have a gas-filled swim bladder like bony fish.

But, there are lots of differences too. Unlike sharks, most rays rest on the sea floor and have eyes on the top of their heads to watch out for predators. Many rays also have thin, whiplike tails, of which some are armed with defensive venomous spines.

In order to breathe, a ray usually takes water in through a large spiracle, or hole, behind each eye. This is just as well, because a ray's mouth faces the

A SOUTHERN STINGRAY SWIMS IN THE CARIBBEAN SEA.

WEIRD WORLD
RAYS EVOLVED FROM SHARKS ABOUT 220 MILLION YEARS AGO. THE EARLIEST KNOWN RAYS LOOKED LIKE SHARKS, AND FOSSILS SHOW THAT SOME WERE SIMILAR TO MODERN GUITARFISH.

sand, and taking in water the usual way could mean getting a sandy mouthful! Water is then passed over the gills, and flows out through gill slits, which are under the ray's flat head – not on its side like a shark.

Swimming along

The biggest difference between sharks and rays is the ray's huge pectoral fins. These extend in a continuous sweep along each side of the head and down the body. Most rays swim by rippling the edges of their pectoral fins in a wave that

Highly mobile

The eagle and cownose rays are agile swimmers. In these rays, their pointed pectoral fins are like wings that beat up and down so they seem to fly through the water. By beating their fins alternately they can turn this way and that to escape hungry sharks.

A SPOTTED RAY RIPPLES ITS PECTORAL FINS TO SWIM.

passes from the front to the back of the fins, propelling the ray forwards.

Rays usually have spindly tails that are not much use for swimming. One exception is the electric ray with its thicker tail that swishes from side to side to help it swim.

Manta rays have the biggest wings of all. They can grow to more than 7.6 m (25 ft) across – that's bigger than a car! These rays are famous for leaping clear out of the water. No one knows why mantas leap but it could be to help them remove parasites from their skin.

48

Where rays live

There are more than 630 species of ray, most of which live in the sea. They can be found in all oceans, from shallow water to depths of nearly 3 km (1.8 miles), and most live on or close to the sea floor. The deepest dwellers are members of the skate family, which are typical rays with diamond or round-shaped bodies and slender tails. Some rays, such as stingarees, venture into estuaries. River rays always live in freshwater, as you can guess by their name.

Finding food

Most rays feed along the sea floor, which is not surprising since their mouths lie under their heads. Like sharks, they have electrosense pores that can help them find hidden food. Once they've located their prey, they capture it in different ways. Spotted eagle rays hunt for clams by probing the mud with their snouts. Cownose rays also use their pectoral fins to clear away sand from a clam or a crab. They then crack open the shellfish with

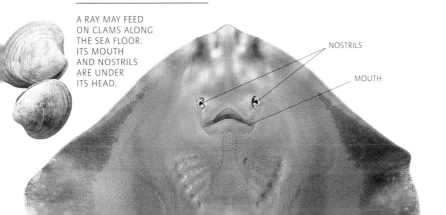

A RAY MAY FEED ON CLAMS ALONG THE SEA FLOOR. ITS MOUTH AND NOSTRILS ARE UNDER ITS HEAD.

NOSTRILS

MOUTH

WEIRD WORLD
THE ATLANTIC TORPEDO RAY CAN PRODUCE AS MUCH AS 220 VOLTS OF ELECTRICITY.

their flat, crushing teeth, swallowing only the juicier morsels.

Shock tactics
Electric rays feed on fish and other creatures that live on or near the sea floor of warm or cool coastal waters. Once the rays come into contact with their prey, they stun it with powerful electric shocks. Electricity is generated in large muscles on either side of their disc-shaped bodies. The blocks of muscles are like a series of

batteries linked together, and are capable of packing a powerful shock! The stunned prey is then guided into the ray's mouth by the pectoral fins. Electricity works for defence too. If you stepped on an electric ray, you'd certainly feel the shock!

Filter feeders
Not all rays are this deadly. Mantas have tiny teeth and filter-feed plankton from the water, just like the whale shark and basking sharks. Mantas have large lobes on their heads to guide a steady stream of plankton into their gigantic mouths as they swim along. Mantas may swim together in big circles through patches of food-rich water.

Social lives
Other rays also congregate where food is good. Cownose rays often swim together, making daily journeys inshore to feed in sandy or muddy shallows. Rays also group together to mate, and most give birth to a small number of pups. However, skates lay large eggs with long curly tendrils that anchor each one to the sea floor.

Sting in the tail

Whether busy being sociable, looking for food, or resting on the sea floor – rays can be at risk from attack. To protect themselves, some have

COWNOSE RAYS SWIM IN A GROUP NEAR THE GALÁPAGOS ISLANDS.

large prickles that run along their back and tail as a body armour. Stingrays have a long whiplike tail, which is armed with one or more spines.

If a stingray is stepped on or attacked it whips its tail around to impale its spines into the flesh of the intruder. The spines can get lodged in the flesh, which is painful enough. But the spines are also loaded with venom that produces a bad reaction, and can make a person feel sick or worse. Stingrays only use their weapons if provoked. Some, such as the southern stingray, are actually friendly, curious creatures that approach divers to find out what's going on.

their snouts. So how can you tell a sawfish from a sawshark?

Take a good look at the sharp end – if you dare! Sawsharks have a pair of

SAWFISH LIVE IN RIVERS AND LAKES, AS WELL AS IN THE SEA.

Chainsaw massacre
Sawfish are not as friendly. These types of ray have a weapon at their front end. The huge snout is equipped with sharp teeth on each side. If a sawfish

feelers, called barbels, half way along the snout. They also have gill slits on the

sides of the head, instead of underneath, like sawfish.

is caught in a fishing net, it can lash out and wound anyone within range. It slashes at fish with its saw to stun or kill them.

Sawfish have look-a-like shark relatives – the sawsharks. They also have a saw on

Guitarfish
Other sharklike rays are the guitarfish, which live in warm coastal waters to depths of a few hundred metres. They are guitar-shaped with a triangular head, roundish

body, and a tail that is broader than is seen in most other rays.

The ones with the broadest tails swim like sharks by sweeping the tail back and forth, while fins on their back act as stabilizers.

Distant cousins
More distant cousins of sharks and rays are chimaeras. On the

IN GREEN SAWFISH, TEETH AT THE TIP OF THE SNOUT ARE CLOSER TO EACH OTHER THAN AT THE BASE.

A SAWFISH DISPLAYS ITS IMPRESSIVE TEETH-LINED SNOUT.

outside chimaeras look nothing like sharks or rays. They have smooth skins, big eyes, and big heads. The first fin on the back can be raised and lowered, and a flap covers their gills, as if hey are bony fish. It's their cartilage skeleton that unites them with sharks and rays.

For defence, chimaeras have a venomous spine on their backs. Most chimaeras prefer deep, cold water but some can be found in the shallows if it is cold enough. There are many different chimaeras, including the plownoses that have a hooked snout for probing the sea floor for food, and

the ratfish that have long, ratlike tails.

Sharks certainly have some interesting relatives whether it's the odd-looking chimaeras or the curious, venomous stingray. For most it is hard to tell they are related but if you looked inside every shark, ray, or chimaera, you'd find that flexible skeleton of cartilage.

A PLOWNOSE CHIMAERA SWIMS OFF THE COAST OF NEW ZEALAND.

VILE VENOM

Sharks and their relatives are not the only fearsome creatures in the sea. Other types of fish can also be harmful. Sea creatures may use venom – a poison that is jabbed into the skin by spines, fangs, or teeth – as a way to subdue their prey or to defend themselves. Some other fish protect themselves by coating their bodies in poisonous slime so that a predator will spit them out. If we handle or step on these creatures they will treat us as enemies.

THIS VENOMOUS SCORPIONFISH IS DISGUISED BY ITS WEEDLIKE APPEARANCE.

Stinging fish

You've just seen that stingrays have one or more spines loaded with venom on their tail. Some bony fish, like the scorpionfish, are also equipped to sting. Their stings aren't in their tail, they're on their fins instead. The dorsal fin on the back of the fish has the most.

Why do scorpionfish need their venom? Most scorpionfish spend their time lying on rocks or corals waiting to pounce on a fish or crab wandering by.

As they lie in wait, a larger fish could easily attack them. So, they need good protection. Their first line of defence is camouflage – they look like weed-covered rocks or corals. Their skin is rough with many ragged projections and its colour is similar to the rocks and corals in which the fish

54

hides. This disguise keeps the scorpionfish hidden from both predators and prey.

A scorpionfish's venomous spines are its second line of defence. At the base of each spine is a sac of venom. If bitten by a predator the venom is squeezed out as the spines penetrate the predator's skin, injecting it with poison. Scorpionfish, and some of their relatives such as the stonefish, have such good disguises that we can't see them, which is why you must never touch anything on a coral reef.

WEIRD WORLD
THE LIONFISH USES THE LARGE FINS ON ITS SIDES LIKE FANS, HERDING SMALL FISH AND SHRIMP AGAINST THE REEF, SO THEY CAN BE CAPTURED AND SWALLOWED.

Stripy lionfish
The most elegant members of the scorpionfish family are the lionfish. They have long venomous spines on their backs that give them excellent protection from predators.

A LIONFISH HAS PROTECTIVE, VENOMOUS SPINES ON ITS DORSAL, PELVIC, AND ANAL FINS.

At night, they hover around coral reefs feeding on small creatures. During the day, lionfish often hide under coral ledges or in rock crevices and hardly move at all. When they swim out from a coral reef, their stripes stand out and serve as a bright warning to predators to keep away! For this reason, they are fearless creatures, and divers can swim very close to them.

Poison and prickles

Porcupinefish are other creatures armed with spines on their body. In some species, the spines stick out permanently, but in others the spines lie flat against the body unless under attack. When attacked they inflate into a spiny ball by swallowing lots of water. A fish or seal trying to eat an inflated porcupinefish will find it difficult to get its jaws around the spiky, balloon-like body.

Pufferfish, as their name suggests, can inflate. Some of them have another trick too. Their liver contains a poison that is around 1,200 times stronger than cyanide. It affects the nervous system of any animal that eats it. Less than a teaspoonful can kill a human.

Incredibly, the flesh from some pufferfish is a delicacy in Japan. The flesh, called fugu, is served at special restaurants where the chefs perform the delicate task of cutting out the most poisonous bits. You would have to trust the chef to eat there!

Spiny skins

People eat all kinds of seafood – even sea urchins! Their roes (eggs) are a delicacy in Japan,

A CHEF PREPARES FUGU. FIRST, HE REMOVES THE POISONOUS PARTS OF THE PUFFERFISH.

France, and Spain. Unfortunately, its coat of needle-sharp spines does little to protect the urchin from humans intent on eating it.

Some urchins can be dangerous to pick up. Grab a black urchin from the Mediterranean Sea and its spines would puncture your skin. Stepping on one would be even worse as the needles can break off in your skin and are hard to remove.

The tropical long-spined urchin is even better equipped, with poison-coated spines that can grow up to 30 cm (12 in). Some creatures have worked out a sneaky way to prey on these urchins. The triggerfish blows water at the urchin to flip it over. It then bites the underneath, where there are fewer spines.

Long-spined urchins provide a safe refuge for other creatures who know their predators won't come near the spines. Razorfish hang about head-down among the spines, their vertical stripes blending in nicely.

Blue for danger
Another venomous sea creature is the blue-ringed octopus.

Although only about the size of a person's hand, the four species of blue-ringed octopus are extremely venomous. They are said to contain enough venom to paralyse 10 people!

The blue-ringed octopus lives in rock pools along the Australian coast and, like all octopuses, has a parrot-like beak. As it bites into prey with its beak, the wound can be flooded with venom-laden saliva. When provoked, the blue rings on its tentacles and body flash more brightly. It's a clear signal that means leave me alone!

THE BLUE-RINGED OCTOPUS IS ONE OF EARTH'S MOST VENOMOUS CREATURES.

Colourful cones

Cone snails are also venomous sea creatures. They have beautifully patterned shells, although you should never touch them or take them from

sharp, curved teeth at the front of the sea snake's mouth. As the snake strikes, the venom passes through the hollow fangs and into the wound of the victim.

Sea snakes live in the tropical

SEA SNAKES CAN CLOSE THEIR NOSTRILS TO KEEP WATER OUT.

a reef. Sea creatures should avoid getting close too! Cone snails have a dart-like hollow tooth, which they jab into their prey. The tooth injects venom so potent that the cone snail can paralyse prey that is larger than itself. The poison affects the prey quickly and it cannot swim away. It is then engulfed by the cone snail's expandable food tube and gobbled up.

Cone snails that feed on fish have stronger venom than those that eat worms or other snails. A few fish-eating cone snails, like the geography cone, can kill people with their venom.

Sea snakes

Of all the venomous creatures in the world, we often think of snakes when it comes to deadly bites. Those that live in the sea have some of the most toxic venom of any snake. The poison is injected through

waters of the Pacific and Indian oceans where they feed on fish. Most sea snakes grow to about 0.5–1 m (1.5–3.3 ft) in length, although some can reach 2 m (6.6 ft). They power along with the help of their paddle-like tail. Sea snakes can dive to 250 m (820 ft) and can stay underwater for long periods on a lungful of air and by absorbing oxygen from the water through their skin into the blood vessels in their heads.

It must be unnerving for a diver to be inspected by a curious sea snake as it swims past! Despite their reputation, however, people are rarely injured by sea snakes.

Whether armed with fangs or spines, sea creatures have to make the best of their weapons to survive in the oceans.

A YELLOW-LIPPED SEA KRAIT SLITHERS OVER A REEF OFF INDONESIA'S SULAWESI ISLAND.

STINGING JELLIES

Jellyfish may look beautiful as they slowly swim along, but beware! Their tentacles are armed with thousands of deadly stings. Jellyfish aren't the only stingers in the sea – their relatives, such as corals, sea anemones, and hydrozoans are also armed. Jellyfish stun or paralyse prey with their stings, which are key to their survival as an important ocean predator.

Swimming bells
Jellyfish have simple bell-shaped bodies made of a squishy jelly-like substance – which is how they got their name. Some are transparent, others range in colour from yellowish-orange to pinkish-purple. Deep-sea jellyfish can even glow in the dark.

To swim, the jellyfish contracts its bell so that water whooshes out and propels the jellyfish along. The bell then returns to its original shape and water rushes back inside ready for the next contraction. Jellyfish are not strong swimmers so are often swept along by currents.

No brain
Jellyfish don't have brains but they do fine without them. A network of nerve cells sends signals around the bell so the

jellyfish can coordinate its movements. On the rim of the bell, gravity receptors tell the jellyfish which way up it is facing, while light receptors let the jellyfish know how far it is from the sunlit surface.

Stinging tentacles

As the jellyfish moves, the tentacles, armed with thousands of tiny stinging cells, trail behind. Each cell is usually equipped with a trigger that is set off by the touch and smell of a passing fish or shrimp. When this happens, the cell turns inside out – like blowing out the end of a rubber glove. As it does so, it shoots out a tiny, threadlike tube, which stabs its victim and releases venom. When hit by many stings, the prey is paralysed. Other cells on the tentacles release threads that stick to or coil around

> ### WEIRD WORLD
> DESPITE THEIR NAME, JELLYFISH ARE NOT ACTUALLY FISH. THEY'RE CNIDARIANS – SIMPLE CREATURES WITH STINGING CELLS. JELLYFISH ARE 95 PER CENT WATER – THEY HAVE NO HEART, BLOOD, BONES, OR BRAIN!

parts of the prey to make sure it doesn't get away after being stung.

Eating prey

Once the prey is stunned and captured, the jellyfish uses its frilly arms to pass the creature up to its mouth. In some types of jellyfish, the tentacles retract, as though they are on a winch, bringing the prey towards the mouth. Digestive juices break

SEA NETTLES, A TYPE OF JELLYFISH, SWIM OFF THE WEST COAST OF THE USA.

down the food into a soupy mass, which is absorbed by the cells in the bell. Indigestible bits are passed out through the same opening. Jellyfish only have one body opening for eating and excreting. Yuck!

Dangerous jellies

Jellyfish mostly use their stings to catch prey, but people can also get stung if they touch one or swim into a trailing tentacle. Not all jellyfish have powerful stings. For example, the moon jellyfish uses mucus to trap its food, so only needs a weak sting.

Jellyfish that swarm in coastal waters are hard to avoid. People often name these stingers after living things that sting

us on land, such as nettles or wasps.

The most deadly jellyfish – the box jellyfish – has a short, simple name that diguises its nasty nature. It lives in warm coastal waters off northern Australia and south-east Asia. Tentacles at each corner trail behind it for up to 3 m (12 ft) and its boxlike bell has sides up to 20 cm (8 in) long. The box jellyfish is virtually see-through so it is hard to spot in the water.

Jellyfish season

To avoid being stung, people are advised not to swim in summer when box jellyfish swarm in coastal waters. Signs at the beach warn bathers not to enter the water. Anyone who gets too close to the box

THIS BOX JELLYFISH MODEL SHOWS A CLOSE UP OF THE DEADLY STINGING CELLS IN ITS TENTACLES.

AS THE STINGING CELL SENSES A FISH BRUSHING PAST, IT SHOOTS OUT A BARBED TUBE.

THE BARB CUTS INTO THE FISH'S FLESH.

VENOM IS INJECTED INTO THE FISH.

CORAL, SUCH AS THIS PIPE-ORGAN CORAL, STINGS AND CATCHES PLANKTON IN ITS TINY TENTACLES.

A settled life

The Portuguese man o' war spends its life adrift in warm waters. Their cousins, the hydrozoans, grow anchored to

MAN O' WAR TENTACLES CAN BE LONGER THAN A BLUE WHALE.

jellyfish will find themselves under attack! Tentacles stick to the skin and are hard to remove without triggering more stings. They are incredibly painful and leave nasty red marks.

Men-at-war

A distant relative of the box jellyfish, the Portuguese man o' war, delivers stings that are so painful you could faint! It is not a single animal but a colony of interconnected organisms called polyps. English sailors named it after the old Portuguese fighting ship – the man-of-war – because its gas-filled float looked like the ship's triangular sail. This float sits up out of the water while leaving leaving the rest of it below the surface. Its long tentacles, which are equipped with nasty stings, find food and are used as a means of defence. The tentacles also haul food up into little stomachs where it is digested. Other parts of the man o' war make sperm or eggs.

surfaces – anything from rocks to piers. They have a bunch of flower-like heads each circled by a ring of stinging tentacles.

Sea anemones also like a settled life although they can creep along on their base. Some even do somersaults to escape being eaten! Like all their relatives, they have stinging tentacles to capture food. Some types of tropical anemone can give a nasty sting.

Coral reef

Unlike squishy jellyfish and sea anemones, hard corals have stony skeletons. It is their skeletons that help make coral reefs – home for many sea creatures. Look closely at a coral and you will see that its tiny colony members resemble mini sea anemones. They get some of their food by capturing plankton in their stinging tentacles. Corals also have tiny, single-celled organisms in their tissues that, like plants, make food using energy from sunlight.

Friends and enemies
Surprisingly, despite their powerful stings, jellyfish and anemones also provide a home for fish. For example, the splendid tentacles of the lion's mane jellyfish shelter some fish. The fish seem to be rarely stung and are safe from larger predators.

Some fish don't seem to be affected when they nibble at an anemone's tentacles.

The beautiful clownfish shelter in large anemones, and secrete a thick layer of mucus that stops the anemone's stinging cells from firing.

Jellyfish and their relatives may be simple forms of life but they have existed in oceans for 700 million years. Stinging tentacles have proved to be just as good a way to catch prey as rows and rows of sharp teeth.

CLOWNFISH SWIM SAFELY AMONG STINGING ANEMONES.

NASTY NIPPERS

Crunch! That's the sound made as a crab, lobster, mantis shrimp, or other crustacean – an animal with a tough, crusty, outer shell – clamps its claws around prey. People can also get a nasty nip – especially if the crab or lobster feels threatened. Their pincers, or claws, have sharp or crushing edges which make them powerful weapons.

Crunching claws
The biggest claws belong to the lobsters – some of the largest crustaceans. The giants of the lobster world grow up to 1.1 m (3.5 ft) long and have two huge claws at the front.

The claws are not identical. One claw – the lobster's crusher – has a knobbly edge like a nutcracker which is used for crushing hard-shelled prey. The other claw, the cutter, has sharp blades

like scissors. The lobster uses it for snipping up soft creatures or dead flesh. Inside, large muscles operate the claws, giving them the strength to kill and pull apart their prey.

Facing a challenge

Lobsters lurk under rocky ledges with their claws facing out, ready to challenge intruders. At night they venture out over the sea floor finding dead or dying animals to feed on. If enemies approach, they can flap their tails to swim away.

A cornered lobster puts up a good fight, waving its claws to show it is well armed. If that doesn't work, the lobster will try to nip the attacker.

Smashing claws

The record for the "fastest claw in the sea" goes to the mantis shrimps. Mantis shrimps shoot out their front claws in a fraction of a second. Some have spiny claws that spear fish and soft prey. Others have club-shaped claws for smashing shelled prey to bits. These mantis shrimps can even break the glass of a fish tank or aquarium.

Mantis shrimps generally live in warmer waters where they lurk in burrows which they have dug out of the sand, mud, or shell material on the sea floor. Fishers that have dredged up these little monsters can get a slashed finger or thumb as they try to get them out of their nets.

Scuttle and swim

Another crusty sea creature with sharp nippers is the crab. Some are good swimmers, with flat, paddle-like back legs. Their other legs are used to scuttle along the sea floor.

The blue crab lives in bays and estuaries along the east coast of North America.

THE COMMON LOBSTER RESTS IN A ROCKY CREVICE. IF AN ENEMY APPROACHES, THE LOBSTER WAVES ITS PINCERS AS A THREAT.

It is a versatile swimmer that can swim sideways, backwards, forwards, and can even hover. Usually found in lagoons and estuaries, it feeds mainly on molluscs, worms, small fish, and carrion. It lives for about two years.

New shells

Like all crabs and their relatives, blue crabs have to shed, or moult, their shells as they outgrow them. The old shell is shed, to make way for the new one which is soft at first. Until it hardens, the crab is easy prey for a predator.

Some crabs, such as the hermit crab, need more protection because their abdomens stay soft all the time. So, to protect itself the hermit crab lives inside an empty sea snail's shell. One claw is bigger than the other and is used to block up the entrance of the shell – just like a front door. When a hermit crab grows bigger, it has to move home. First, it finds a bigger shell. Then it carefully examines the shell's opening, size, and weight and, if suitable, it quickly moves in.

Protection and camouflage

Hermit crabs like having guests. They may put sea anemones on their shells to hide from and ward off predators. A fish trying to devour a hermit crab may get a mouthful of stings instead. The anemone benefits too by

feeding on particles of food that the crab drops.

While some hermit crabs have anemone friends, sponge crabs like sponges. Not that sponges can sting but they do help the crab hide from enemies such as large fish and sharks. The crab uses its claws to snip the sponge into just the right shape to cover its body.

Others, such as the decorator crab, put bits of seaweed on their shells, hoping they will grow to give them camouflage. Claws are handy tools and

WEIRD WORLD
MANY MALE CRABS USE THEIR CLAWS IN COURTSHIP DISPLAYS. THE MALE FIDDLER CRAB ATTRACTS A FEMALE INTO HIS BURROW BY WAVING HIS LARGER CLAW.

good weapons for crustaceans. Their crusty shell is useful as armour – but it has a drawback. It has to be shed as it grows leaving the lobster, mantis shrimp, or crab vulnerable until the new shell hardens.

BLUE CRABS EAT DECAYING AS WELL AS FRESHLY DEAD FISH. THEY ALSO PREY ON OTHER CRUSTACEANS, BIVALVES, AND MARINE WORMS. THEY USE THEIR CLAWS TO HOLD AND BREAK UP FOOD ITEMS

MONSTERS OF THE DEEP

DRAGONFISH LIVE IN THE OCEAN DEPTHS.

The sea has always inspired myth and mystery. For centuries, little was known of its depths or the strange creatures that lived there, and frightening encounters with bizarre sea beasts led to far-fetched stories. Today, there is still much of the deep sea to explore and lots more to discover about sharks and other sea creatures.

Shark stories

People like stories about sharks whether they've met one or not. Such is their influence that traditional stories from Pacific Islanders tell of sea gods that could magically change from a person into a shark and back again. In some Pacific cultures, boys had to catch sharks as part of their rite of passage into manhood.

Today, blockbuster films really grab our attention. *Jaws*, the film made in 1975, is a classic thriller

about a rogue great white shark intent on eating people. A scary, but invented, story!

Sea serpents

Among the favourite monsters of old were sea serpents. These dragonlike monsters were shown in paintings and talked about in sailors' stories. But could a real creature have given rise to these legendary beasts?

One likely candidate is the oarfish which boasts a silvery, ribbon-like body 11 m (36 ft) long. It has a flaming crimson fin on its back, and long fin rays on top of its head. The oarfish is rarely seen as it usually lives at great depths. It feeds on plankton, krill, and squid so it is hardly a monster!

Another possible source of inspiration for sea serpents is the frilled shark. This shark has a long body, a snakelike mouth, and rarely comes to the surface. Unusually, the frilled shark has six pairs of frilly-edged gill slits, and these give the shark its name. Seafarers

SAILORS INVENTED SEA SERPENT TALES TO ACCOUNT FOR LOST SHIPS.

A SEA SERPENT OR A FAKE? THIS PHOTO WAS TAKEN IN THE USA, IN 1906.

THE ANGLERFISH
HAS SHARP TEETH
AND A LUMINOUS
LURE TO ATTRACT PREY
IN THE DARK DEPTHS.

may have seen this shark for many years before scientists studied it in the late 1800s. Corpses of basking sharks have certainly been mistaken for sea serpents.

Tentacle tales

When it comes to monsters, those with lots of legs can be scary! Think of octopuses and squid, then imagine them the size of a ship. Hey presto, you have a corker of a monster. The kraken, a creature from Norwegian mythology, was just such a monster. Some drawings show the kraken with eight legs like an octopus.

As far as real octopuses go, the giant octopus from the north Pacific Ocean is the biggest. It grows to nearly 9.8 m (32 ft) across, from tentacle tip to tentacle tip. If touched, the giant octopus may give a diver a friendly embrace, but it is unlikely to do much more than pull out a diver's mouthpiece.

Giant squid

It is more likely that a giant squid was mistaken for being the kraken. The giant squid is big, VERY big, growing up to 13 m (43 ft) long. It also has the biggest eyeballs of any living creature!

THIS HATCHET FISH MODEL SHOWS IT HAS LARGE EYES TO SEE IN THE GLOOM.

Although the giant squid has been known to scientists since the late 1850s, our knowledge was limited to dead specimens washed ashore or brought up from the deep ocean in fishing nets. It was eventually photographed in its natural environment in 2004 and filmed in 2012.

Monsters in the deep

Deep-sea fish fit the role of scary monsters perfectly because they look so weird. Some look evil due to their large mouths lined with daggerlike teeth. They have appropriate names such as dragonfish, hatchet fish, or anglerfish. There is not much food in the dark, cold depths. So when a meal does come along, some deep-sea fish with wide-opening mouths and stretchy stomachs swallow prey that is larger than themselves.

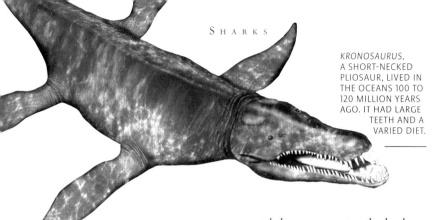

KRONOSAURUS, A SHORT-NECKED PLIOSAUR, LIVED IN THE OCEANS 100 TO 120 MILLION YEARS AGO. IT HAD LARGE TEETH AND A VARIED DIET.

Lights in the dark

As the deep sea is so dark, many fish living there use light to find prey. The stoplight loosejaw, which is also known as the rat-trap fish, does this with red light, as it cannot be seen in deep water. As a result, the light is invisible to the fish's predators and prey cannot see it and run away.

Megatooth

Some of the scariest sea monsters ever are no longer with us – they're extinct. So there's no chance you'll meet one! Among the extinct sharks, the most alarming is the *megalodon*, or megatooth shark as some like to call it. Scientists have found fossils of their teeth that show a *megalodon*'s tooth is at least twice the size of a great white's. Now think of rows and rows of these teeth, and a huge set of jaws, and that's hair-raising!

The *megalodon* is only known from its teeth and vertebrae. Scientists used to think that it was most closely related to the great white but it now seems that, among living sharks, it is more closely related to the mako shark. Along with its large size, tooth marks on bones attributed to *megalodon* suggest it fed on dwarf whales and seals. Luckily for us, it became extinct just over three and a half million years ago.

Giant sea reptiles

The last of the giant sea reptiles disappeared about 66 million years ago – at the same time as the dinosaurs became extinct on land. The biggest of these sea reptiles were the pliosaurs. These hefty beasts paddled through the ocean, hunting other sea creatures. Pliosaurs had enormous jaws lined with sharp teeth, so

Loch Ness they'd have to surface for air. So why is the monster so rarely seen?

Sea monsters, whether based on reality or not, are just good fun. Searching for

THE BIGGEST *KRONOSAURUS* TEETH WERE 25 CM (10 IN) LONG.

could take large chunks out of their prey.

Loch Ness or not?
Long, slender-necked plesiosaurs also swam in the sea. Some could turn their necks rapidly sideways to catch prey. Plesiosaurs are one source of inspiration for the Loch Ness monster, reputed to live in a deep lake (loch) in Scotland. In the 1930s, a fake head, looking much like that of a plesiosaur, was photographed as a hoax in Loch Ness. If there were plesiosaurs in the depths of

the truth about monsters can inspire us to look further into the sea's untold mysteries.

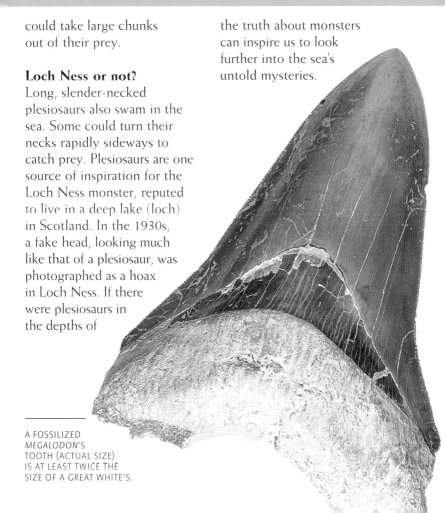

A FOSSILIZED
MEGALODON'S
TOOTH (ACTUAL SIZE)
IS AT LEAST TWICE THE
SIZE OF A GREAT WHITE'S.

OCEANS AT RISK

The world's oceans are teeming with life – from top predator sharks to the tiny plankton that drift on the surface. All of these sea creatures form part of a chain of feeding links – made up of predators and prey – known as a food chain. Human activities have upset this delicate balance and they are now in danger of putting the ocean itself at risk. There are, however, things we can do to help.

Sharks at the top

Sharks help maintain the balance of life in the sea. They have an important position as top predators in the food chain. If the number of sharks is reduced then this has a knock-on effect all

SHARKS EAT LARGE FISH, SUCH AS COD.

BIG SHARKS ARE AT THE TOP OF THE FOOD CHAIN. AS ADULTS, THEIR MOST DANGEROUS PREDATOR IS PEOPLE.

the way through the feeding links. Sharks help keep other marine populations in check, which helps to sustain the right balance of predators and prey at each level in the chain. Sharks may also pick off diseased animals in a group which keeps a population healthy. They also provide a clean-up service by eating the remains of dead creatures.

MANY FISH EAT PLANKTON – THE LOWEST LINKS IN THE CHAIN. PLANTLIKE PLANKTON, LIKE THESE DIATOMS, USE THE SUN'S ENERGY TO MAKE FOOD.

Studying sharks

Scientists are gradually learning more about the importance of sharks. Some of what we know comes from

COD EAT SMALLER FISH, SUCH AS HERRINGS.

studying them in aquariums. Increasingly, however, sharks are studied in the wild where divers can observe their behaviour in a natural habitat.

Some individual sharks, such as great whites and basking sharks, can be recognized by their scars and markings. Their behaviour can then be recorded using hand-held or remote-controlled video devices and cameras.

Tagging

One way to gather information on shark migration is to attach an identification tag to their dorsal fins. The tag then sends the research team radio or satellite messages at regular intervals that give the exact location of the shark. Other

A CARIBBEAN REEF SHARK IS RELEASED AFTER BEING TAGGED.

A TIGER SHARK IS CAUGHT IN A BEACH NET OFF DURBAN, SOUTH AFRICA.

methods involve aerial searches, using drones or helicopters to record shark movements, and more recently, using underwater devices attached to natural features projecting from the sea floor. These pick up signals from tagged sharks as they pass along their migration routes. Even gathering pieces of shark DNA by filtering it from the seawater can reveal information about shark movements and their numbers. Tracing sharks helps scientists find out where they spend their time, which, in turn, helps to conserve them.

Sharks at risk

For many reasons sharks are more at risk from us than we are of them. Hundreds get caught in beach nets put up to protect swimmers from sharks in South Africa and Australia. Sharks are also caught by anglers, people who hunt large fish for sport.

A FLEET OF FISHING BOATS ANCHORS OFF DASSEN ISLAND, IN SOUTH AFRICA. OVERFISHING IS A BIG THREAT TO SHARKS AND OTHER SEA LIFE.

However, the biggest threat to sharks and other sea creatures is commercial fishing that is driven by our demand for the products sharks provide us with. Many millions of sharks and their cartilaginous relatives are caught each year for food. You may be surprised to learn that the "rock salmon" used in British fish and chips is actually dogfish, a shark. Their cartilage and liver oil are also used in industry and for making medicines and cosmetics.

Overfishing
The breeding patterns of sharks make them especially vulnerable. They may take up to six years to reach breeding age and even then may only produce a few pups during heir lifetime. They are being fished faster than they are replaced, making their numbers fall rapidly. A number of species are endangered, some are very endangered, and others are likely to go extinct.

WEIRD WORLD
SHARK FINS ARE HIGHLY VALUED IN SOME ASIAN COUNTRIES FOR SHARK FIN SOUP. SHARKS ARE KILLED JUST FOR THEIR FINS, OR ARE LEFT TO DIE ONCE THE FINS HAVE BEEN CUT OFF.

Other types of sea life, such as lobsters and sea cucumbers, are suffering the same fate. Careful monitoring of species, the creation of "no fishing" zones, restrictions on catches, and changing the mesh size of fishing nets can help to maintain fish numbers and protect young individuals. But this does not prevent illegal fishing. Shark fin soup is a delicacy in many Asian cuisines and it is a major contributor to the millions of sharks that are killed each year.

By-catch
Sharks and rays can also be caught by accident when fishers are trying to net other types of fish or they are longline fishing. The unwanted

SCUBA DIVING IS A GREAT WAY TO
SEE UNDERWATER LIFE, BUT CARELESS
DIVERS CAN DAMAGE CORAL IF THEY
KICK THE REEF WITH THEIR FINS.

water starves the coral of
sunlight that is crucial to
their growth.

catch, called by-catch, is
wastefully dumped overboard.
Some trawlers throw back
40 per cent of their catch –
dead or dying. When sawfish,
which are endangered, get

Warming waters
Coral is also sensitive to
the rise in water temperature
being caused by global
warming. This can stress
coral, causing it to whiten –

OVER 100 MILLION SHARKS AND THEIR RELATIVES ARE CAUGHT EVERY YEAR.

caught in nets, they are often
killed because they're hard
to untangle.

Wrecking reefs
Illegal fishing methods
can also damage coral reefs,
which are home to many
sharks and other sea creatures.
In Southeast Asia, some fishers
dynamite reefs and then simply
collect dead fish from the
surface. Others use the poison
cyanide to collect reef fish for
the aquarium trade and live
tanks in restaurants. Cyanide
squirted into the reef's nooks
and crannies temporarily
confuses the fish, making
them easy to catch. Reefs can
also be ruined if soil washes
into the sea from building sites
or badly farmed land. Cloudy

known as bleaching – and shut
down for periods during the
summer months. A permanent
temperature rise would kill
the coral and the animals
that depend on it for survival.
Rising temperatures are also
causing sea ice to disappear,
which causes problems for
animals such as polar bears
and penguins, which live
in polar regions.

Nasty chemicals
Pollutants, such as industrial
chemicals and metals, also find
their way into the sea via rivers.
Others, such as raw sewage,
may be piped directly onto
beaches and into the sea. This
damages sea life, especially if
these pollutants get into the
food chain. As these pollutants

UNTREATED WASTE WATER POURING
OUT OF A PIPE INTO THE OCEAN

the food chain. Pollutants can also affect the development and growth of creatures or make them prone to disease.

Oil spills

We can't see most sea pollution but oil spills are impossible to hide. These happen when supertankers or the oil rigs themselves leak oil into the surrounding seas. Oil that floats on the top of the water can poison animals that swallow it. Seashore creatures can be smothered by the oil and suffocate. It also damages bird

pass along a food chain, from one organism to the next, their concentration rises slowly. It is highest in the top predator of

feathers and seal fur, making them lose their waterproofing and causing death. The toxic effects of an oil spill can also cause a food chain to break down if the animals in one of the links are badly affected or die out, or the environment itself is seriously degraded for a while.

Load of rubbish

Another problem affecting sea life is rubbish disposal. Everything from nuclear waste and abandoned fishing tackle to batteries and household items can be found in our

oceans. Some of it causes serious problems for marine life. Plastic is a major problem as there is so much of it. It is estimated that there are at least 5.25 trillion pieces of plastic in the ocean where it can float close to the surface or sink to the sea floor. Some particles are so small that we can't see them with the naked eye. These microplastics can be eaten by marine creatures and passed up the food chain. Scientists are studying what effects these microplastics might have.

Get involved

Despite the gloomy outlook, our oceans can be saved if we all work together. As we learn more about the behaviour of marine animals and their role in keeping the ocean healthy,

VOLUNTEERS HELP CLEAN UP A SPILL FROM AN OIL TANKER, *JESSICA*, NEAR THE GALÁPAGOS ISLANDS IN 2001.

our attitudes towards them are changing. This is particularly true of the large predators, such as sharks and whales – many of these are now protected by law.

If you want to see sharks and other sea creatures, visiting an aquarium is a good idea. These are good places to start to learn about sea life, and how to get involved in conservation work. Find out about places you can visit, and conservation groups you can join, at the end of this book. Everyone can do things to help look after the sea and its amazing creatures.

What you can do

• Find out about the sea and its creatures to understand why they need protection.

• Walk along the seashore with someone who'll tell you about sea life. Look at critters lurking in rockpools and at shells on the beach. If you like watching marine creatures, remember that crabs and fish left in a bucket die. Look at creatures but always put them back where you found them.

• Take your rubbish home from the beach. Buried litter soon comes back to the surface. Be aware that plastic can kill. The plastic rings that hold cans of drink together are particularly dangerous. Cut through the rings so they can't strangle sea creatures if you accidentally drop them.

• Don't touch or step on corals. It damages them, and can cut or sting you.

• Never buy souvenirs made of coral, shells, or sharks' teeth.

• Recycle. This can also save energy – especially recycling aluminium cans because mining and processing aluminium uses lots of energy. Recycling also cuts down the amount of rubbish that needs to be disposed.

• Save energy. Wear a jumper made of natural fibres instead of turning the heating up. Walk or cycle instead of taking the car. This way, we can cut down the amount of fossil fuels transported or burned.

VOLUNTEERS TAKE PART IN A BEACH CLEAN-UP IN CAPE TOWN, SOUTH AFRICA.

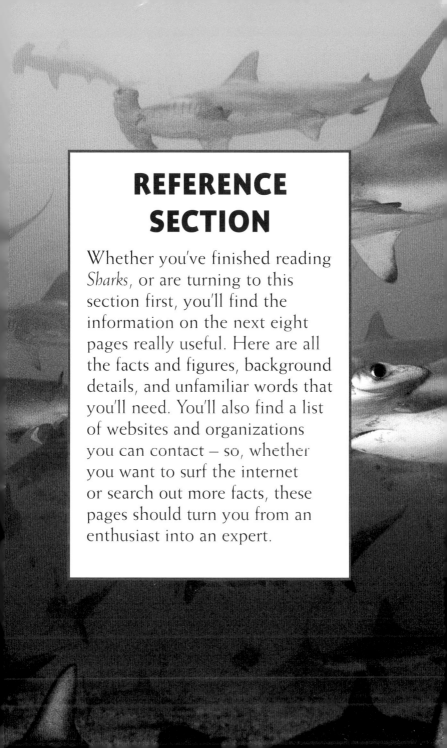

REFERENCE SECTION

Whether you've finished reading *Sharks*, or are turning to this section first, you'll find the information on the next eight pages really useful. Here are all the facts and figures, background details, and unfamiliar words that you'll need. You'll also find a list of websites and organizations you can contact – so, whether you want to surf the internet or search out more facts, these pages should turn you from an enthusiast into an expert.

CLASSIFYING A SHARK

Sharks, like all animals, are classified into different categories that are based on features that they share. The largest category is the Domain – there are three of these: Bacteria, Archaea, and Eukarya. Domain Eukarya has six kingdoms – including Animalia, the one that all animals belong to. The kingdoms are divided into smaller and smaller categories until you get to individual species, which are identified by a feature or features that are unique to that species. Sometimes categories are subdivided again, for example, into subclasses (see opposite). The chart below shows the classification of the shortfin mako shark.

Kingdom: Animalia
This group includes organisms that obtain energy from feeding on other living things or their remains. Most are multicellular and reproduce sexually.

Phylum: Chordata
This group includes organisms that have a flexible rodlike notochord at some stage of their life. All vertebrates belong to this phylum.

Class: Chondrichthyes
This group includes organisms that have a skeleton made of cartilage.

Order: Lamniformes
This group includes organisms that have two spineless dorsal fins, and a mouth that extends back beyond the eyes.

Family: Lamnidae
In the animals in this group, the blood is warmed by retention of muscle heat. This family includes the great white, porbeagle, and salmon sharks.

Genus: *Isurus*
This genus includes two species – the longfin and shortfin mako sharks.

Species: *oxyrinchus*
The species is the shortfin mako. Its pectoral fins are two-thirds the length of its head.

What is a species?
A species is the basic unit of classification. A species is a group of similar animals that are capable of breeding together in the wild to produce fertile offspring.

KEY SHARK AND RAY ORDERS

Scientists classify sharks, rays, and other fish into groups according to the features they share.

Fish

Fish with jaws

Jawless fish

Class Chondrichthyes – cartilaginous fish
Have skeletons made of cartilage.

Class Osteichthyes – bony fish

Class Cephalaspidomorphi – lampreys, hagfish

Subclass Elasmobranchii – sharks, rays
Don't have the upper jaw fixed firmly to the braincase, and have gill slits.

Subclass Holocephali – chimaeras

Shark Orders

Ray Orders

Hexanchiformes – frilled sharks, cow sharks

Torpediniformes – electric rays

Echinorhiniformes – bramble sharks

Rhinopristiformes – sawfish, guitarfish

Squaliformes – dogfish sharks, including gulper sharks and lantern sharks

Rajiformes – skates

Heterodontiformes – bullhead or horn sharks

Myliobatiformes – stingrays, eagle rays, manta rays

Orectolobiformes – carpet sharks, including the whale shark and wobbegongs

Carcharhiniformes – ground sharks, including requiem sharks and hammerhead sharks

Lamniformes – mackerel sharks, including the basking shark, the goblin shark, and thresher sharks

Pristiophoriformes – sawsharks

Squatiniformes – angel sharks

SHARK RECORDS

Biggest shark
• The whale shark is the biggest shark and also the biggest fish in the sea. The males grow at least 6 m (19.7 ft) long and the females grow at least 8 m (26.2 ft) long.

Smallest shark
• The dwarf lantern shark is the smallest shark. The males grow 160–170 mm (6.3–6.7 in) long and the females grow 190 mm (7.4 in) long. Other small sharks include the pygmy ribbontail catshark (24 cm [9.4 in] long) and the spined pygmy shark (25 cm [9.8 in] long).

Biggest predator
• The great white shark is the biggest shark that hunts for prey. It grows more than 6 m (19.7 ft) long, and weighs two tonnes.

Most dangerous to people
• Great whites have made 326 unprovoked attacks on humans since 1876. This amounts to only 2 or 3 attacks on humans per year.

Biggest tooth ever
• The extinct *megalodon* shark had teeth about 18 cm (7 in) high from the base to the sharp tip.

Longest tail
• Thresher sharks have tails almost as long as their bodies.

Widest head
• The winghead shark has a head whose width is nearly half the length of its body.

Longest lived
• The greenland shark can live to at least 272 years.

Deepest living
• The cookiecutter may swim from depths of about 2–3 km (1.24–1.86 miles) to the surface at night.

Fastest
• The shortfin mako is probably the fastest, with some reputed to reach bursts of speed of 68 kph (42.25 mph) or faster.

Longest migration
• A great white called called Lydia travelled 20,000 km (12,427 miles) across the Indian ocean.

Breeding rates
• The sand tiger and the bigeye thresher give birth to only two pups at a time.
• The whale shark carries up to 300 embryos at one time.

Longest pregnancy
• Basking shark pups can take up to 3.5 years to develop inside their mother.

Most endangered and least known
• The river sharks are the rarest and least known sharks. They are threatened because they live in a small habitat (compared to the sea) which is under pressure from development.

RAY RECORDS

Biggest ray
• The giant manta ray is the biggest with a wing span up to about 7 m (23 ft), and a weight of up to 2,000 kg (4,409 lb).

Smallest ray
• The short-nose electric ray grows to about 10 cm (4 in) across.

Deepest living
• The pale ray (a type of skate) lives nearly 3 km (1.9 miles) down.

Most electric
• The torpedo electric ray can generate up to 220 volts of electricity.

Most endangered
• More than 70 per cent of rays have disappeared in the last 50 years. The most affected are sawfish, guitarfish, and wedgefish.

Breeding rates
• The lesser electric ray has only two pups at a time.
• The torpedo ray gives birth to up to 60 pups at one time.

OTHER SEA CREATURE RECORDS

Most venomous
• The sea snake can kill an adult with a minute dose of venom. The Dubois' sea snake is the most venomous of all.

Biggest animal without a backbone
• The giant squid is the biggest, with the largest one recorded at 13 m (43 ft) long and weighing nearly a tonne.

Biggest animal with a backbone
• The blue whale is the biggest animal that has ever lived on Earth. It can grow up to 32.6 m (107 ft) long.

Widest legspan
• The Japanese spider crab has a leg span of almost 4 m (13 ft).

Heaviest lobster
• The American lobster can grow more than 1 m (3.3 ft) long, from its claws to the tip of its tail, and weighs up to 20 kg (44 lb).

Deepest living fish
• Abyssobrotula, a deep-sea fish, has been taken from depths of more than 8 km (5 miles).

Largest jellyfish
• An Arctic lion's mane jellyfish found washed up on the shore had a bell 2 m (7 ft) wide, and tentacles 36 m (120 ft) long.

Fastest fish
• Sailfish have reached speeds of 110 kph (68 mph).

OCEAN ORGANIZATIONS

Marine Conservation Society
UK-based charity that involves
people in projects including beach
clean-ups. Visit their website
for great information on marine
wildlife and the environment.
Overross House
Ross Park
Ross-on-Wye
Herefordshire HR9 7US
www.mcsuk.org
E-mail: info@mcsuk.org

The Coral Reef Alliance
Promotes coral-reef conservation
worldwide by supporting
protection efforts and raising
public awareness.
1330 Broadway, Suite 600
Oakland
CA 94612
USA
www.coral.org
E-mail: info@coral.org

The Shark Trust
The Shark Trust promotes the study,
management, and conservation of
sharks, skates, and rays. Shark Focus
magazine has photographs,
information, and the latest shark
conservation news. You can even
adopt a shark!
The Shark Trust
4 Creykes Court
The Millfields
Plymouth PL1 3JB
www.sharktrust.org

WWF-UK
WWF is the world's largest
conservation organization.
Visit their website to check
out what the UK branch is

doing for marine conservation.
The Living Planet Centre
Rufford House
Brewery Road
Woking
Surrey GU21 4LL
www.wwf.org.uk
E-mail: supportercare@wwf.org.uk

OTHER USEFUL WEB LINKS:

Environment Australia
Good information on sharks,
Australian marine conservation,
and links to other websites.
https://www.environment.gov.au/
marine/marine-species/sharks

Extreme Science
Find out all sorts of fun
facts and figures in the
"Animal Kingdom" section
on this website.
www.extremescience.com

FishBase
A database with detailed information
on sharks and other fish.
www.fishbase.org

**IUCN's Red List (International
Union for Conservation of Nature)**
To find out more about endangered
and threatened sharks and rays
go to their website and search under
the name of the shark or ray.
www.iucnredlist.org

KwaZulu-Natal Sharks Board
The Natal Shark Board services
shark nets along beaches in South
Africa. It has an education
programme on safe swimming,

and the biology of sharks.
www.shark.co.za

NOVA online
Stacks of shark information.
Also stories of people's close
encounters with sharks.
www.pbs.org/wgbh/nova/
sharks/world/

**San Diego Natural History
Museum**
Plenty of photographs, and facts
and figures about sharks.
http://archive.sdnhm.org/kids/
sharks/index.html

**The Pelagic Shark Research
Foundation**
Useful information on sharks.
www.pelagic.org

WildAid
This US-based, non-profit
organization is currently
campaigning against shark
finning and overfishing.
https://wildaid.org/programs/
sharks/

VISIT AN AQUARIUM

If you want to see sharks, rays, and other sea creatures, or you'd like to learn
more about marine conservation, you might enjoy a visit to an aquarium:

Monterey Bay Aquarium,
California, USA
www.montereybayaquarium.org/

National Marine Aquarium,
Plymouth, UK
www.national-aquarium.co.uk

Nausicaá Aquarium,
Boulevard Sainte-Beuve, 62200
Boulogne-sur Mer, France
www.nausicaa.fr/

New England Aquarium,
Boston, USA
www.neaq.org

Oceanário de Lisboa,
Lisbon, Portugal
www.oceanario.pt

Oceanogràfic,
Valencia, Spain
www.oceanografic.org/en/

Océanopolis,
Port de Plaisance du Moulin Blanc,
29200 Brest, France
www.oceanopolis.com/en/welcome

SEA LIFE London Aquarium, UK
https://www.visitsealife.com/london/

SEA LIFE Sydney Aquarium, Australia
www.visitsealife.com/sydney/

Seattle Aquarium, USA
www.seattleaquarium.org

The Deep, Hull, UK
www.thedeep.co.uk

GLOSSARY

Barbels
Feelers on the tip of a shark's or other fish's snout. Used to feel or taste food.

Basihyal
A flap of cartilage on the floor of the mouth of sharks. It is referred to as their "tongue".

Bony fish
A group of fish with bony skeletons, overlapping scales, and a flap covering their gills.

Buoyancy
The ability to stay afloat.

Cartilage
A tough, flexible tissue that makes up the skeleton of sharks and rays. Can be strengthened by minerals.

Chimaeras
A group of cartilaginous fish related to sharks and rays but with only four pairs of gills.

Claspers
A paired structure next to the pelvic fins of sharks and rays that transfers sperm into the female's cloaca.

Cloaca
A body opening used for both reproduction and passing out waste.

Courtship
Actions of a pair of animals that encourage them to mate.

Crustacean
A group of mainly aquatic animals, such as crabs and lobsters, with jointed legs and a tough outer covering.

Cyanide
A poison used by people to temporarily paralyse fish.

Denticles
Toothlike scales on a shark's skin. These give skin a rough texture.

Electrosense
The ability of sharks and rays to detect weak electric signals and magnetic fields produced by other organisms.

Embryo
A developing baby animal before birth or hatching.

Estuary
Where a river flows into the sea and the water is a mixture of seawater and freshwater.

Excreting
Passing out wastes.

Feeding frenzy
A group of sharks feeding so competitively that they may even bite each other.

Fertilization
When a sperm meets an egg and a new life begins.

Fin spines
Single spines in front of one or both dorsal fins of some sharks, such as horn sharks. Spines also occur on several fins of other fish, such as scorpionfish.

Food chain
A way of looking at who eats what. In oceans they begin with plankton or algae and end with top predators, such as sharks.

Gills
Thin-walled structures containing blood vessels that allow fish to breathe by absorbing oxygen from the surrounding water, and passing out carbon dioxide.

Gill rakers
Bristlelike structures on the sides of the gills of sharks and other fish that sieve water passing to the gills. Used in basking sharks to filter plankton.

Gill slits
Openings on the side of a shark's head, or underside of a ray, through which

seawater exits after oxygen is extracted by the gills.

Habitat
A place where an organism lives.

Iris
The coloured part of the eye. It surrounds the hole called the pupil.

Lateral line
A line of sensory organs along the sides of a shark and other fish. They have cells with tiny hairs that detect vibrations of other animals among other things.

Light receptors
A group of cells that can detect light.

Mermaid's purses
The horny egg cases of certain types of shark and ray.

Migrate
To make a seasonal round trip from one area to another – often for feeding and breeding.

Mucus
In fish, a slippery, stringy fluid produced by the skin for protection.

Nutrients
Substances that maintain life and fuel an animal's growth.

Overfishing
Catching more fish than can be replaced by those that are left, so the population declines.

Parasites
Organisms that feed on, or in, other organisms causing them harm.

Pectoral fin
Paired fins on the side of the body just behind the head.

Pincers
Claws on crab, lobster, or other crustacean mainly used to cut, crush, or pick up food.

Plankton
Small organisms that drift in water.

Pollutants
Harmful substances that contaminate the air, water, soil, or food.

Pupil (eye)
In sharks, the dark area in the centre of the iris that controls the amount of light entering the eye.

Scavengers
Animals that feed on dead animals or waste.

Shark pups
The young of sharks after birth or hatching.

Species
The basic unit of classification that defines a group of organisms that share many features and which can breed with one another.

Spiracle
An opening behind the eyes of a shark or a ray through which it can take in water to breathe.

Submersible
Crewed or uncrewed underwater vehicle that can carry researchers and/or their equipment to great depth. Some are operated remotely. **Swim bladder**
A gas-filled structure in bony fish that helps them control their buoyancy.

Tagging
Attaching a numbered tag to a shark or other animal. Some tags have the ability to transmit signals.

Tentacles
Long flexible structures around the mouth of jellyfish, anemones, and squid.

Umbilical cord
A flexible tube-like connection between an unborn shark baby to its mother's blood supply.

Venom
A poison produced by an animal and injected or jabbed into another animal by a sting or a bite.

INDEX

ACKNOWLEDGMENTS

The publisher would like to thank the following people for their help with making the book:

Marcus James for initial design concept, Robin Hunter for design assistance, Shanker Prasad for DTP assistance, Priyanka Sharma and Saloni Singh for the jacket, Caroline Stamps for proofreading, and Chris Bernstein for the index.

DK Photography by:

Geoff Brightling, Jane Burton, Andy Crawford, Michael Dent, Philip Dowell, Andreas Einsiedel, Neil Fletcher, Steve Gorton, Frank Greenaway, Colin Keates, Dave King, David Murray, Brian Pitkin, Steve Shott, and Harry Taylor.

DK illustrations by:

Ann Winterbotham and Dominic Zwemmer.